KEEPING YOUR HEAD UP WHEN YOUR JOB'S GOT YOU DOWN

KEEPING YOUR HEAD UP WHEN YOUR JOB'S GOT YOU DOWN

DOUG SHERMAN

Wolgemuth & Hyatt, Publishers, Inc.
Brentwood, Tennessee

The mission of Wolgemuth & Hyatt, Publishers, Inc. is to publish and distribute books that lead individuals toward:

- A personal faith in the one true God: Father, Son, and Holy Spirit;

- A lifestyle of practical discipleship; and

- A worldview that is consistent with the historic, Christian faith.

Moreover, the Company endeavors to accomplish this mission at a reasonable profit and in a manner which glorifies God and serves His Kingdom.

Unless otherwise noted, all Scripture quotations are from the New American Standard Bible, ©1960, 1962, 1963, 1968, 1971, 1972, 1973, 1975, 1977, by The Lockman Foundation and are used by permission.

Wolgemuth & Hyatt, Publishers, Inc.
1749 Mallory Lane, Suite 110
Brentwood, Tennessee 37027

Library of Congress Cataloging-in-Publication Data

Sherman, Doug.
    Keeping your head up when your job's got you down / Doug
Sherman.— 1st ed.
      p. cm.
    ISBN 1-56121-041-2
    1. Work—Religious aspects—Christianity. 2. Job stress—
Religious aspects—Christianity. 3. Job satisfaction—Religious
aspects—Christianity. 4. Attitude (Psychology)—Religious aspects—
Christianity. I. Title.
BT738.5.S55 1991
248.8'8—dc20
                                 91-8327
                                   CIP

To my wife, Jan,
whose warm and gentle spirit
brought wisdom when I was criticized,
faith when I doubted,
trust when we faced financial uncertainty,
and strength through her
belief in me and in the career calling
He has given us.
In the most difficult hours of our career,
she reminded me to be "strong and
courageous" (Joshua 1).
Without her support
my head would not be up today.

CONTENTS

Acknowledgments / *xi*

Introduction / *1*

Part 1: Opportunity Knocks

1. Opportunity Knocks / *9*
   Faces of Pain / Common Ground / Summary / Review / Study or Discussion Questions / For Personal Reflection

2. What You Can't Learn in Sunday School / *21*
   Repositioning Christ in Our Lives / Changing Our Perceptions of Life / Using the Chance to Practice Truth / The Benefits of Being a Good Learner / Four Things a Good Student Must Do / Review / Study or Discussion Questions / For Personal Application

Part 2: A Changed Attitude Comes from a Changed Character

3. Skydiving Without a Parachute: Not Recommended / *39*
   Three Dreams We All Have / If Only I Can Become a Competitive Person / If Only I Can Be Competent / If Only I Can Be a Consumer of Luxury Items / Why Pursuing Ego Goals Brings Anger, Stress, and Ultimately Emptiness / C'mon! What's Wrong with Career Achievement? / Review / Study or Discussion Questions

4. Introducing Your New Boss / *59*
   Your Work Should Be Seen as an Extension of God's Work / Your Work Should Be a Service to Others / Your Real Boss Should Be Jesus Christ / Review / Study or Discussion Questions

5. Riding the Roller Coaster of Personal Significance / 77

Your Choice—One Judge or Many? / True Significance Comes from Accepting God's View of You / Personal Significance Is Given to You as a Gift / Your Faith May Have to Override Your Feelings / Going Deep / Review / Study or Discussion Questions / Optional

6. Holding Your Career with a Light Touch / 95

Thank God for What You Have Rather Than Complain About What You Lack / Remember God's Previous Faithfulness to You / Implore God for His Help Today, and Keep Your Focus on One Day at a Time / Accept God's Right to Direct the Events in Your Life / Leave the Future to God / Seek Christlike Character More Than Comfort and Convenience / Review / Study or Discussion Questions / Optional

Part 3: With a Changed Attitude, You Can Take the Right Action

7. Your Second Family / 117

God Wants You to Love Them! / "I Care" Philosophy / Seven Principles of Conflict Resolution / Be a French Horn, Not a Clanging Cymbal / Review / Study or Discussion Questions / Optional

8. Difficult Relationships / 135

The Difficult Boss / The Difficult Co-Worker or Client / We All Go on to Our Reward / Review / Study or Discussion Questions

9. Conquering Stress Before It Conquers You / 151

There I Was at Thirty Thousand Feet . . . / Ego Stress: Going the Wrong Way on a One-way Street / Holding on too Tightly / Time and Responsibility Stress / Owing a Debt to Society / When Your Tank Is on Empty / Stressed for Success / Review / Study or Discussion Questions

10. Really Enjoying Your Work / 167

Choices / To Enjoy Your Work Fully, You Must Enjoy the Lord / To Enjoy Your Work, You Must Have a Compelling Vision of What You Do and Why You Do It / To Enjoy Your Work, You Must Be Realistic About the Fact That You Are Not Going to Change the World / To Enjoy Your Work, You Must Be Realistic About Work and the Fruit of Your Work / To Enjoy Your Work, You Must Be Realistic About the Length of Your Life / To Enjoy Your Work, You Must Be Realistic About Your Shortcomings / To Enjoy Your Work, You Must Work on a Positive Attitude / To Enjoy Your Work, You Must Celebrate Life and Enjoy Family and Friends / A Change in Circumstance or a Change in Attitude? / Review / Study or Discussion Questions

11. Diagnostics / 185
    The Lost Art of Biblical Wisdom / Three Steps to Biblical Wisdom / What Do You Do When You Are in a Boring or Unchallenging Job? / How Can You Keep a Good Attitude when the People Around Do Not? / What Do You Do When the Work Is Never Done? / When Should You Leave Your Job? / What Do You Do When Your Best Was Not Good Enough? / What Do You Do When You Have Made a Big Mistake? / What Do You Do When You Are a Woman in a Man's World? / How Do You Keep Your Motivation High in the Face of Cutbacks and Pay Cuts? / What Do You Do When You Face Midlife Disappointment? / What Do You Do When You Have Lost Your Job? / Review / Study or Discussion Questions

Part 4: Honoring Christ Under Pressure

12. Heroes / 205
    Ordinary People / Extraordinary Character / The Reward of Glory / The Reward of Responsibility

Appendix: A Thirty-Day Plan to Help You Honor Christ at Work / 215

Subject Index / 221

Scripture Index / 225

About the Author / 227

ACKNOWLEDGMENTS

I would like to thank some of my mentors in Christ, Drs. Jerry White, Howard Hendricks, Norman Geisler, Elliott Johnson, and Leroy Eims. My thinking has been shaped by the writings of many, including C. S. Lewis and Dr. A. W. Tozer. I am grateful to Dr. Larry Crabb for his excellent works that enhanced my understanding of some material in chapter 3.

Because I have come to value having a scaffolding of friends to keep me on course and Christ-centered, I would like to mention a few. Dr. Max Anders, Ron and Peggy Bower, Tim Brookshire, Bob Buford, Jeff and Debbie Bond, Randy and Jill Brandt, Mike Cahill, Mike and Janice Chadwick, Doug Coe, Dr. David and Debbie Dalton, Jim and Carol Dethmer, Bob and Lil Fulton, Paul Hansen, Dr. Wayne Hey, Doug Holladay, Dr. John and Mary Isch, Fred and Marilee Laughlin, Robbie and Judy Linn, Gordon MacDonald, Dave and Diane Mayfield, Don and Sally Meredith, Howard Morrison, Charlie and Suzanne Olcott, Al and Kathleen Pirozzoli, Terry and Gail Prindiville, Bill Reichel, Mike and Beverly Reilly, Scott and Shelley Rosenthal, Don Schmaltz, Dr. Dave and Helen Schmidt, Steve and Becky Scott, Pete and Diane Sutton, Frank and Cathy Tanana, Richard Wewerka, Trey and Paula Yarbrough.

I see this book as a team project. I would like to thank our very special friend Ray Bandi for his thorough and thoughtful editing of the book. Thanks also goes to Scott Rosenthal, Ray Blunt, and Ray and Marlene Glenn for their help and suggestions. Special thanks to Charlie Olcott and Terry Prindiville, two busy executives who took the time to read and recommend this book to you and did it on short notice. I am deeply grateful to Mike

Hyatt and his talented editorial staff, including Russ Sorensen and Donna Sherwood.

I have been greatly blessed with wonderful parents, Dick and Mary Lee, with my wife Jan, along with three very incredible children, Jason, Matthew, and Jennifer. They are great!

INTRODUCTION

*No man has any right to offer advice
who has not first heard God speak. No
man has any right to counsel others who
is not ready to hear and follow the counsel of the Lord. True moral wisdom must
always be an echo of God's voice. The
only safe light for our path is the light
which is reflected from Christ, the light
of the world.*

Dr. A. W. Tozer

This book is my second choice of method for presenting this material to you. My first choice would be to sit down over a cup of coffee and to share these ideas with you personally or at least to work with you directly in one of my seminars. You see, the content of this book has been forged like steel in the white hot heat of my own struggles in honoring Christ at work. The lessons of this book reveal my personal experience with the Lord over the years. I have faced nearly every work struggle in this book, but over the last two years I have been through a concentrated program of learning. Never in my life have I felt so much like a personal failure. Let me explain.

Seven years ago, my wife and I started a ministry to people in the workplace in the Dallas area. The early years saw rocket growth, budget increases, several publishing contracts, a daily radio program in two hundred cities, and a video program used in churches across the country. Then came the oil-banking-real-es-

1

tate crash. Ninety percent of our donor base eroded in eighteen months. We let people go, reduced our ministry services, and stopped the radio program.

Personally, each day we wondered if we would continue. For years we had believed that a dream would come true, and then it looked as though it would die. It seemed we were about to lose all our personal money in the effort to keep things going. I blamed myself for everything that had happened, and there were some who agreed. Financial uncertainty, breathtaking stress, feelings of failure were common. But every day God seemed to speak to me, and I kept a record of these thoughts. Ironically, many of the truths I had been teaching were underscored in a new and deeper way.

Today, I feel like a different person from the one I was three years ago. Jesus Christ has become more personal to me. Significant character issues were raised, and change is taking place.

Although we saw the edge of the cliff many times, the organization, Career Impact Ministries, did not die. But its survival and continuance have taken on new meaning. My head is up, and I am not discouraged.

This book presents the sacred truths that kept me going and gave me the perspective on my work that allowed me to have joy in the midst of pain and sanity in the midst of chaos. It is my best attempt to give you a crisp and articulate understanding of what I learned.

But because of what these lessons have meant to me, the message of the following pages is sent to you with a passion that I hope you can feel—and maybe even warm your hands by. While what I've written is very personal, it is not biographical. It is organized systematically, moving from biblical fundamentals to practical application.

THE POINT OF THIS BOOK

The central theme of this book is to help you really enjoy your work by making Christ the center of each workday. Certainly I can't promise to make your specific job situation "heaven on earth." What I can say is that going through work difficulties can reposition Jesus Christ in your life. When He is at the center, He can bring lasting joy and fulfillment in tough times.

"The central theme of this book is to help you really enjoy your work by making Christ the center of each workday."

Our Lord has given us so much encouragement in the Scriptures, my goal is to do some digging for you to help you apply the truths of God's Word to practical work problems.

AN OUTLINE

There are four major parts.

Part 1, "Opportunity Knocks," focuses on God's use of pain and adversity to teach us His ways and to reposition the person of Christ in our lives. Commonly, we want to know why we are facing less than an ideal life: "What did I do to deserve this?" This section is committed to addressing the purpose of what you face and how you can gain the most from your experience.

Part 2, "A Changed Attitude Comes from a Changed Character," addresses mandatory character issues that form the basis for emotional relief from the struggles we face. Unlike so much of the self-help material in bookstores today, there is no simple formula to reduce stress and enjoy work. We all wish we could be microwaved and come out with a fresh new attitude toward work and life, an attitude that would bring continual happiness. But real change comes somewhat more slowly. It requires that we look at the world through different glasses, that our drives and motivations become purified, and that Jesus Christ become a more significant part of our workday experience. But these changes are possible! There is hope! You can change, and you can keep your head up!

Part 3, "With a Changed Attitude, You Can Take the Right Action," addresses specific issues and problems with biblical wisdom. The work world is filled with conflict, stress, and difficulty. This section will offer specific advice and Scripture for some of the most common problems you face. After nearly a decade of speaking and answering questions on how Christians can apply their faith to their work, I will discuss the most often raised questions and issues.

Part 4 will wrap up the book with "Honoring Christ Under Pressure." This section will look at people who have kept their heads up in tough job situations.

From the outset I would like, in a way, to develop a relationship with you. I care about the struggles you face. I want to be a help and encouragement to you. I want to lead you to greater joy in Christ. You are not alone.

HOW TO GET THE MOST FROM THIS BOOK

First, realize that the principles and ideas here require some real thought. The opportunity before you to grow and change is exciting! Real change does not come quickly or easily. But it can come! Here are three ideas on how.

Read this book with a pen, and mark up the margins. Add your own thoughts. By all means, record how all this is affecting you personally. Remember, the book contains little about how you can change your circumstances. Most is on how you can change yourself to deal effectively with the circumstances in which you find yourself. Perhaps you would like to read the book through quickly and then come back and mark it up.

Second, plan to do the exercises at the end of each chapter. *You will double the book's value to your life by doing so.* The danger of information without application is that it simply makes us smarter sinners. If possible, *find a friend or a group of friends to do these exercises with you.* Their insights and comments can *greatly* enhance what you get out of the material.

Finally, be realistic. Real change does not happen overnight. Neither do humans achieve perfection in this life. Think of your life as a baseball player thinks of his career. A .300 batting average is considered great. That means that he only gets a hit three out of every ten times at bat. Many Christians feel that they must bat 1.000 to be considered acceptable to God. Not true!

I have grown a lot as I have tried to follow the ideals of this book. But every day is a new day for me. Sometimes I follow my own advice; sometimes I don't. My hope for both of us is not perfection. It's simply progress.

My hope is that through the study of this book Jesus Christ will become a more dynamic part of your life, that you will learn to really enjoy your job, and that you will:

Keep your head up when your job has got you down.

PART 1

OPPORTUNITY KNOCKS

— I

OPPORTUNITY KNOCKS

Difficult circumstances often create paradigm shifts, whole new frames of reference by which people see the world and themselves and others in it, and what life is asking of them.

STEPHEN COVEY

O ver the past decade, I have interacted personally with a myriad of people facing all sorts of work issues. The emotional spectrum ranges from the excitement of a promotion and the thrill of a sale to crippling stress, bitterness, anger, and frustration beyond expression. There are both the good and the bad— a lot of bad. But every difficult experience offers a unique opportunity to grow and change.

FACES OF PAIN

Let me share with you a few accounts of people and the work difficulties they face. Imbedded in each of these cases is an opportunity to grow. As you read their accounts, ask yourself what you think they could gain from their circumstance and also how you think they might solve their dilemmas and keep their "heads up."

While some of the names and details have been changed to protect their privacy, these are real individuals.

Karen

I had just completed a seminar on the Christian in the marketplace, titled "Your Work Matters to God," at a Christian conference in a large East Coast city. During this time we discussed why God had given us work, practical ways to honor Him, and how to face some of the severity of the tough secular work world. After I spoke, a large group came up to talk about particular issues they were facing. An attractive woman in her mid-thirties patiently waited for the crowd to leave. She had little animation in her face and obviously was more than mildly bothered.

With a deadpan face, Karen described her situation to me. For the last fifteen years she had taught in a middle school. She felt that God had called her to teaching to make a difference in the lives of young children. Normally I would have interrupted her to tell her how proud I was that she could see work the way God sees it, but her face told me I had only heard the good news of a good news-bad news story.

Her real dream was to be a school principal, and she had poured fifteen years into teaching, giving lots of extra hours to extracurricular activities to enhance her chances. Last year at a Christmas party for teachers and administration, her principal struck up a conversation with her about the true meaning of Christmas. As a follower of Christ, she took the opportunity to share the good news of Christ's birth and the offer of eternal life in Him. Again, I was very proud of her.

But her eyes began to squint with pain and her lips became tight. I just listened. She went on to say that the principal at the party became very angry with her. He didn't need a savior. He hadn't done anything wrong; certainly he wasn't like so many hypocrites who went to church. From this point on, the principal seemed to have it in for her. With long pauses she explained that he gave her a relatively low performance rating two months later. It was the first rating that was not outstanding in fifteen years.

Almost choking she said that the rating came out just as she was under consideration for principal at a nearby school. The low rating cost her the job she had worked so hard for, the job she felt God had called her to do. With misted eyes she asked, "Doug, how can I overcome the anger and hatred I feel toward this man? I have trou-

---

"Every difficult experience offers a unique opportunity to grow and change."

---

ble sleeping, and my life seems ruined. What do I do?" She was a wounded soldier of the marketplace, victimized by injustice.

But what could she gain from this? How could she maintain a good attitude? Let's consider another individual and his situation.

Jack

I fly a fair amount to speaking engagements at seminars and conferences on the Christian in the marketplace. Recently, as I was flying from Dallas to my home near Washington, D.C., a fellow who worked for a major hotel chain was sitting next to me. He was well dressed—a four-hundred-dollar suit, suspenders, wire-rimmed glasses—you know the type. He exuded ambition. Perhaps he was twenty-five, flying high in the Washington singles scene. I asked him how things were going, and he said they were going great and gave every indication that he was on his way to the top. I'm sure he thought I was impressed. Of course I was. I understood since not that many years ago I was on a similar track in the Air Force, young and unsure of who I was with much to prove.

Perhaps I erred by asking him about the reorganization of his company that had headlined the business section of the paper for the week before this flight. He paused for a minute, looking at his shoes, and said that he was not sure what would happen to him. The company had sold many of its hotels, an entire chain of restaurants, and its most profitable subsidiary. It was obvious to Jack that he was not indispensable. He was clearly scared but had trouble admitting it, saying something innocuous like "whatever will be, will be." I really hurt for him. He made it clear that he did not have a personal relationship with Christ and that his only real source of personal significance was in doing well in his career. Now that his job was in jeopardy, his worth as a person was too. Apparently my little probe and a friendly face led him to tell me that he had no real savings and that he would be in real trouble if he lost his job. Jack was feeling very threatened. His job, his significance, his reputation among his peers, his social life were all on the chopping block, and, worse, he felt helpless to do anything about it. All he could do was wait, trapped in a Russian roulette game, to see if he would be the next victim.

But what opportunity would you see for him? How would you suggest that he stay encouraged?

Let me tell you about one more individual, and then we will explore the issue of "opportunity knocking."

Jim

Jim was an excellent mechanic who took great pride in his work. He told me that what he did, he did for Christ. He wanted to please the Lord with the quality of his work. He worked faster and harder than the other guys in his shop. If a customer needed a car fixed that day, Jim volunteered to stay after hours to fix it.

But the other employees resented him. He made them look bad, and they returned the favor by making his life miserable. At night they took his tools. During the day, they stole his lunch box. He was the butt of jokes, and because of his faith they took special delight in plastering calendar girl pictures near his work area. At breaks he was clearly considered an outsider, which left him feeling lonely and frustrated. He thought of quitting, but that seemed to be giving in. Yet working there was miserable.

Again, what are your thoughts on his opportunity? Should he not work as hard? What would you suggest?

All of us have different ways of coping. I call some of the most common responses "common ground."

COMMON GROUND

People's response to pain is telling. Most people see pain as their enemy and either try to pretend it's not there or wallow in help-lessness as though they have no recourse. We feel victimized by outside forces beyond our control and are convinced the real problem is with the system or with others. As with all victims, we are convinced we don't deserve the pain and are angry about it. People who feel this way are on common ground.

Here are some common examples. See if you can relate to any of them.

Bitterness

I hate snakes. One day when I was in Southeast Asia, I went to a snake farm because my friends wanted to see it and I wanted to be with them. It was pretty disgusting. The feature attraction was a cobra pit with some cobra handlers who played flutes and made the snake stand up and sway to the music. I learned later how deadly these snakes were. One gram of their venom can kill 165 people!

Often when people face work struggles, a toxic poison, like the cobra venom, forms inside them. We call it bitterness. It slowly eats away at their souls and poisons everyone around them. Bitterness could start with the boss, a client, or manage-ment. But once it begins, it can injure innocent bystanders. It can ruin a marriage, injure children emotionally, and sour friend-ships. Worse, bitterness is rarely recognized by the bitter. Their smoldering anger engages them whenever they are not involved in a peak concentration event. In the shower, all they can think about is that crummy boss, the insulting co-worker, and so on. As they drive down the road, this toxic acid begins to sour the mo-ment, fuel anger, and seek methods of revenge.

Such low- to high-voltage anger affects every intimate rela-tionship. We kick the dog, yell at our spouses, gripe at everything the kids do, and generally make everyone feel that we are a volcano about to erupt at any time. Don't mess with us!

Frustration with God

Common ground includes getting angry at God for not serving us better. You can hear the complaint, "God, haven't I served you well? Haven't I given my money and time? I know I am so much more godly than _____!"

We hear biblical truths about His goodness and power and we become skeptical. When we hear a testimony of a person who is intoxicated with a newfound relationship with Christ, we want to throw up.

The psalmist in Psalm 77 reflects his frustration with God in the following questions.

> Will the LORD reject forever?
> And will He never be favorable again?
> Has His lovingkindness ceased forever?
> Has His promise come to an end forever?
> Has God forgotten to be gracious?
> Or has He in anger withdrawn His compassion?
> (Psalm 77:7–9)

It is common to respond to the pain of work by being frustrated with God. Other people find escape hatches.

Escape Hatches

Common ground includes looking for escape mechanisms to dull our pain or divert our attention long enough for temporary pleasure to interrupt the frustration, anger, and fear. Here are some escape hatches that are commonly used.

- television as a drug
- alcohol/drugs
- overeating
- pornography
- immoral sex or sexual fantasies

All these, of course, open the door for evil to come in and create worse discouragement than before. They invite an invisible force into your life whose only purpose is *your* destruction. Picture a serpent behind each one of these, reminiscent of the one in Genesis 1, saying, "Just escape for a while. Don't face your problems. Pain is bad for you, so enjoy momentary pleasure. Maybe tomorrow things will get better. You've suffered a lot—you deserve to enjoy yourself!" And this monster of evil with red sulfu-

---

"The number one thing you can change is your attitude and your response to what you are facing."

---

rous breath smiles as you are drawn into his trap.

I am serious when I tell you that I believe demons are behind such strategies! Yet many people fall into these deceptive escape hatches in response to pain.

Becoming Detached and Dictatorial at Home

Common ground for spouses or parents includes being distant and detached from other family members. Often parents become dictatorial, barking out orders so kids will ease the work load and reflect well on their parents.

When these people are at work they are at work; when they are home they are at work. Spouses often feel a kind of emotional adultery going on when a husband or wife actually would rather solve work problems than have intimacy at home. They feel their partner becoming distracted and sometimes catatonic.

Friends and family feel ignored.

It's common for pain to move people to be detached and dictatorial even regarding those they love the most.

Depression

Anger at a boss or the system or even ourselves can turn to self-hatred. This is called depression. We start wearing dark glasses that see the dark side of everything. As we lose motivation, life becomes a chore and a bore.

Again it is common for the depressed person to blame others for "making me depressed." It is not uncommon for depressed people to wonder if life is really worth living. They can get caught in a cycle of self-pity, souring relationships, and then greater depression.

Pain commonly leads to depression.

SUMMARY

There is little self-respect for those who stand on common ground. Misery may love company for a moment, but the fraternity of those who live on this turf gives little comfort. But where do you go for answers? Specifically, where does the Christian go for answers?

Opportunity Knocks

Okay. Let me say it, and then I'm going to duck. What you are now going through could be the best thing that ever happened to you. Yes, I really believe this and am in good company with many who would agree.

Surely, people in difficult circumstances don't want trivial or trite answers. But what I am saying is not trivial. One of the most profound truths taught in the Bible is that positive change takes place through the difficult experiences of life (James 1:2–4; Romans 5:3–5). Trials can be the best thing that ever happened to you because they can bring about positive change.

So many people I have talked to about their problems can only see how *other* people are wrong and how their circumstances must change. The problem is with others, they say. In part, they may be correct. But you can't change other people. Often our circumstances are not nearly as injurious to our well-being as *our response* to those circumstances.

**"To change your attitude,
you must pursue character change."**

If you want to obtain a good perspective in the midst of trials, you must accept the fact that some things about you must change. The way you see yourself, the way you see Christ and His involvement in your career, and the way you relate to people can all change for the better as a result of work difficulties.

The number one thing you can change is your attitude and your response to what you are facing. My neighbor and I have an unspoken rule. We only mow the grass on our own side of the fence. If his yard looks crummy, that is his responsibility. I have my yard and he has his. Life is like this. Some things are my responsibility, and other things belong to my neighbor or others.

- You can't make an angry, self-centered boss be as thoughtful, caring, and fair as Jesus Christ. You can work on your attitude though.
- You can't always make work flow at a nice even pace without pressure. You can learn to relax amid such stress.
- You can't take ultimate control over the destiny of your career and finances. You can learn to be content in any circumstance.
- You may not be able to pick any career you want. You can learn, however, to bring real dignity to and see lasting significance in whatever you do.

Your attitude, however, is simply a reflection of your character. To change your attitude, you must pursue character change. I am talking about a change from the inside out. To respond well to the ups and downs of everyday work requires a *character transformation*. All of us need such an inside-out change. We all need to learn how our inner world can be touched by Jesus Christ so that we respond appropriately to the events that come our way.

If we were cars, we would recognize that we need more than a wax job, more even than an oil change. We need a complete engine and transmission overhaul! Applying a few simple self-help formulas to our lives is like putting wax on a car with an engine completely rusted out. Real change that is lasting and permanent can only be found in Jesus Christ!

Would you like to be content in your circumstances? Would you like to diffuse your anger, to be more caring, to have more meaning and satisfaction? The solution is in *character transformation* found only in a dynamic relationship with Christ.

Opportunity knocks for all of us right now to learn all we can from our work circumstances and allow Christ to change us from the inside out.

In the next chapter, we will focus on how work can be a schoolhouse and how you can be a good student who learns the most from the lessons that come your way.

REVIEW

Main Idea: What you are going through could be one of the best things that ever happened to you. Opportunity knocks!

Key Points:

- There is a lot of pain out there. You're not alone.
- Common responses to work struggles include:
    1. bitterness
    2. frustration with God
    3. escape mechanisms such as
        a. alcohol as a drug

b. television as a drug
c. pornography
d. overeating
e. immoral sex or sexual fantasies
4. detached or dictatorial relationships at home
5. depression

- The most important thing you can focus on is your attitude and your response to what you are facing.
- Your attitude is a reflection of your character. To change your attitude, you must pursue character change.

STUDY OR DISCUSSION QUESTIONS

Part One
(20–30 minutes)

Consider each of the individuals in the first part of the chapter. What advice would you give to each person (Karen, Jack, Jim)?

Part Two
(20–30 minutes)

Which one of the following is the greatest stressor in your life right now? Rank order these from one to seven as relative stress-inducing factors for you, one being the highest stress-inducing factor and seven being the lowest.

☐ conflicts with clients or co-workers

☐ frustration with the boss or management

☐ stress from the work load

☐ lack of meaning or purpose in your job

☐ impossible time demands

☐ feelings of insignificance

☐ insecurity about the future

What makes the two items you ranked highest so stressful?

Part Three
(10 minutes)

Answer the following questions:

1. What can you add to the list of unhealthy diversions you see people using to cope with their jobs?

2. Why is character change necessary to have a good attitude in the midst of work trials?

FOR PERSONAL REFLECTION

1. What are your emotions toward your job right now?

2. How do you feel toward God when you are in the midst of current difficulties at work?

3. What would you say is the impact of your job stress on your family? Are you detached and/or dictatorial at home?

4. Are you looking to any of the following to help you deal with the pain you feel?

   - alcohol
   - drugs
   - television
   - immoral relationships
   - pornography

5. If so, how much do they help?

6. Study the following passages and write down the reasons God brings trials into our lives: James 1:2–4; Romans 5:3–5; 1 Peter 1:6–9.

— II

WHAT YOU CAN'T LEARN IN SUNDAY SCHOOL

I will instruct you and teach you in the way which you should go; I will counsel you with my eye upon you. Do not be as the horse or as the mule which have no understanding, whose trappings include bit and bridle to hold them in check.

PSALM 32:8–9

M any people think that the only thing they receive from work is a paycheck, some measure of fulfillment, and a few headaches. Many Christians think of church as the primary place to learn about the Christian life. Both are wrong.

Your workplace is your schoolhouse. You will spend most of life working. According to a recent study, the average male works 57.1 hours a week, counting his commute time. With eight hours of sleep per night, this means that over half your waking hours are spent at work, which makes your workplace one of the most important arenas in which God can develop your character.

Behind the events of our workday, God has developed a curriculum. Whether we are aware of it or not, He is either the architect of the events of the day or has given evil the permission to deliver difficult circumstances for our good. It is the school of becoming Christlike. In this school you will learn qualities like those listed in Galatians 5:22: "But the fruit of the Spirit is love, joy, peace, patience, kindness, goodness, faithfulness, gentleness, self-control. . . ."

If you study the lives of the Old Testament heroes—Joseph, Daniel, Moses, Job, Abraham, David, Solomon—you will see how God used workplace struggles to teach them what they couldn't learn in Sunday school.

Consider the career path of Joseph, ultimately one of the most powerful men of the ancient Near East world. Here is his resumé.

- Born to a wealthy family.
- At seventeen, his brothers sold him to slave traders.
- Sold to the captain of Pharaoh's guard.
- Does well and gets responsible position.
- Boss's wife comes on to him, he rejects the advance, and she saves face by crying rape.
- Goes to jail, wins trust of guard.
- In jail does a little dream interpretation on the side and gets known to Pharaoh.
- After a short consulting contract with Pharaoh, he is appointed superintendent of the royal granaries, second only to Pharaoh.

I hope you and I can have a little different career path! But one thing will be the same: God's primary interest is in our character, not our career status.

You see, the coin of the realm in God's kingdom is character—Christlike character. In other words, in His economy, He places no value on money, status, or achievement in the eyes of man. Instead, these are just fool's gold, shadows of the real thing. Real gold is the quality of a person's character that reflects Christ's character. Unless and until we realize this, we cannot hope to understand His ways and purposes in our lives. But when we do come to understand, we find meaning and even joy in work difficulties. Paul writes, "And not only this, but we exult in our tribulations, knowing that tribulation brings about perseverance; and perseverance, proven character, and proven character, hope; and hope does not disappoint" (Romans 5:3–5).

It is simply a necessary part of developing our character that we go through the white heat of trials. In that process, impurities are removed, and good character is practiced, refined, and developed.

At this point, you may be wondering what kind of trials are in store for you. Or you may be asking why God would allow you to face difficulties in the first place. This book was written to help you answer these questions. Let me start by painting in some broad brush strokes an explanation of God's allowing difficulties to occur. I've observed three key changes that God wants to make in our lives, changes that will not happen unless we undergo trials.

REPOSITIONING CHRIST IN OUR LIVES

Let's be honest. While Christians have a certain level of love for Christ, most of us are independent people who tend to rely on ourselves and pursue whatever goals we want.

Recently I bought a gas grill on sale at a hardware store. The catch was that I would have to put it together. After two hours and four Tylenol, I decided to look at the directions. I hate to use them—so much that only when I'm exhausted do I look to the manual for help. I am a stubborn, self-reliant person.

When it comes to our relationship with God, we tend to have the same disease. We pray when we feel we have to. We depend on Him only when we are afraid or sense things out of control. C. S. Lewis said it very well.

> Everyone has noticed how hard it is to turn our thoughts to God when everything is going well with us. We "have all we want" is a terrible saying when "all" does not include God. We find God an interruption. As St. Augustine says somewhere, "God wants to give us something, but cannot, because our hands are full—there's nowhere for him to put it." . . . We will

not seek [happiness] in Him as long as He leaves us any other resort where it can even plausibly be looked for. (*Problem of Pain,* Macmillan, New York, NY, 1962, 96)

Lest you begin to feel bad that you must go through pain and frustration to learn to trust Christ, you'll notice that the early church leader, the Apostle Paul, went through the same program.

> For we do not want you to be unaware brethren of our affliction which came to us in Asia so that we were burdened excessively beyond our own strength, so that we despaired even of life; indeed we had the sentence of death within ourselves, in order that we should not trust in ourselves but in God who raises the dead. (2 Corinthians 1:8–9)

We all tend to seek our own glory rather than His. We tend to make Him the caboose in our lives, which is driven by the locomotive of whatever we want. Trials can reestablish a healthy relationship with the Savior. In fact we may not even know that this relationship needs repair, but our heavenly Father knows. Trials readjust our thinking about who He is, who we are, and what is the difference. Trials also remind us that we are in need of the Savior every day to save us from our own bad attitudes and responses and to empower us to be like Him. Only when we come to the end of ourselves do we come to Christ.

CHANGING OUR PERCEPTIONS OF LIFE

We need the same kind of help to change our perception of what life is all about. Remember the automobile example. I said that if we were cars, we would need more than a wax job; we would need an entire overhaul. Let me explain.

Every one of us has a certain kind of glasses through which we see life. We look through these mental glasses at events, people, and our environment. Life, as we look at it, raises some rather deep issues, including some of the following.

- what you expect from work and others
- your perception of your self-worth

- your deepest fears
- your ambition

Our perceptions of life are formed around such issues. But our perceptions can be wrong. When a person comes to Christ, a lot of changes take place. At first outward behavior changes. As new believers we become more honest and more loving. But in

---

"Only when we come to the end of ourselves do we come to Christ."

---

time our perceptions must go through many transformations at the deepest level.

Have you ever met a person who has recovered from a terminal illness? Is that person's perception of life different? Ask him what matters. Have you heard of a very wealthy person who has lost everything? For some it was cause for suicide; others have said it was the best thing that ever happened to them.

Some things in life are "big fish." Others are "little fish." Knowing the difference is perspective.

But it is more than perspective. It goes as deep as our fundamental drives. It is as deep as the unspoken drives of our souls, drives that emerge from some subterranean level in our mind. God wants to change these drives, and he cannot do it while we are in a hammock sipping lemonade. Only in trials will such deep issues emerge.

In this schoolhouse, God wants to purify unhealthy motives, desires, values, and ambitions. We all have them, but they must go.

Pain evaporates the fog and shows us more clearly who we are, who He is, and the difference between the two. The experience can be bittersweet.

USING THE CHANCE TO PRACTICE TRUTH

Like the Greek philosophers who held that pure knowledge is salvation, Christians commonly delight in Bible knowledge alone and believe that "the more they know, the more they grow." But what the Bible actually teaches is that knowledge alone only makes one proud and arrogant (1 Corinthians 8:1). As God conceives it, Christian education is not primarily a formal classroom experience. God's on-the-job training program demands the practice of His truth and principles.

It's one thing to know what Jesus says about forgiveness. It is another for Karen (chapter 1) to forgive the principal who ruined her chances for promotion. As a muscle grows through exercise, so do our souls.

But how does a person learn to be forgiving? Or how do we become patient or persevering or forbearing? Some Christlike characteristics can only be developed through trials. Only when we have been wronged can we learn forgiveness. We will never learn patience unless we have something to endure. God brings trials into our lives to teach us to practice the positive character qualities He has outlined in His Word.

Every time you apply a principle or commandment from God's Word, you put a brick in a building of Christlike character. Progress is slow, but over the years God will use the person who builds this way to reflect His image to a skeptical, secular world. On the other hand, the Christian who simply becomes a smarter sinner, having only greater knowledge, will think more highly of himself than he ought to think.

Even if your work problem today does not contain a purifying factor for you, it still contains the opportunity for you to grow. And some growth can only happen through trials.

So God wants to use the difficult circumstance of life to produce positive changes in us.

- to reposition Christ in our lives
- to change our perceptions of life .
- to give us a chance to practice truth

And as God brings about these three significant changes, we will begin to experience four benefits.

THE BENEFITS OF BEING A GOOD LEARNER

Most of us long for contentment in our souls. We don't want to ride a roller coaster of emotions based on the ups and downs of our work lives. Instead we want to sense real significance that can

---

"God brings trials into our lives to teach us to practice the positive character qualities He has outlined in His Word."

---

never be threatened. We want to have unfailing relationships that we will not have to worry about.

Inner Peace

Rudyard Kipling seems to aspire to the higher ground of inner peace in the following poem.

If

If you can keep your head when all about you
　　Are losing theirs and blaming it on you,
If you can trust yourself when all men doubt you,
　　But make allowance for their doubting too;
If you can wait and not be tired by waiting,
　　Or being lied about, don't deal in lies,
Or being hated, don't give way to hating,
　　And yet don't look too good, nor talk too wise:

If you can dream—and not make dreams your master;
　　If you can think—and not make thoughts your aim;
If you can meet with Triumph and Disaster

And treat those two impostors just the same:
If you can bear to hear the truth you've spoken
    Twisted by knaves to make a trap for fools,
Or watch the things you gave your life to, broken,
    And stoop and build 'em up with worn-out tools:

If you can make one heap of all your winnings
    And risk it on one turn of pitch-and-toss,
And lose, and start again at your beginnings
    And never breathe a word about your loss;
If you can force your heart and nerve and sinew
    To serve your turn long after they are gone,
And so hold on when there is nothing in you
    Except the Will which says to Them: "Hold On!"

If you can talk with crowds and keep your virtue,
    Or walk with Kings—nor lose the common touch,
If neither foes nor loving friends can hurt you,
    If all men count with you, but none too much;
If you can fill the unforgiving minute
    With sixty seconds' worth of distance run,
Yours is the Earth and everything that's in it,
    And—which is more—you'll be a Man my son!

Although this poem is not directly a Christian piece, it contains many of the ideals of a Christian who is clearly living on "higher ground." Christ wants to give you this kind of higher ground contentment. But it will take more than a poem. Paul said that for him, it did not come naturally. He had to become a good student in the very schoolhouse we are discussing. He got contentment the old-fashioned way; he learned it.

> Not that I speak from want; for I have learned to be content in whatever circumstance I am. I know how to get along with humble means and I know how to live in prosperity, in any and every circumstance I have learned the secret of being filled and going hungry, both of having abundance and suffering need. (Philippians 4:11, 12)

Intimacy with Christ

In addition to contentment, your work trial can bring a new intimacy with Christ. When things are tough, we slowly figure out that Christ is our only faithful and true friend.

In his book *When Everything You Ever Wanted Isn't Enough,* Harold Kushner tells the story of watching a couple of kids building a sand castle, an elaborate structure with bridges and towers. Before they finished, a wave came over the beach and destroyed their beautiful castle. The author expected tears. Instead, the children laughed and walked away holding hands—off to build another in another spot. Why? To them the key factor in their happiness was their relationship. Most of us, however, care too much about our sand castles. We worry about the waves that threaten our fragile dreams. We sweat the small stuff and are nonchalant about the important stuff.

But when the castle is washed away, the person there for you is Christ. His hands then seem pretty big. As you draw close to Him, you can feel pretty successful no matter how much money or career achievement you have lost.

It seems that only when we come to the end of self do we come to Christ. He stands there ready and eager for us to have a more intimate relationship with Him.

Imitation of Christ

I am sure you already know some of the joy of experiencing real change in your character. The highest and noblest thing any man or woman can aspire to is to reflect the character of Jesus Christ. Inside of the heart of a follower of Christ is this idea that the coin of the realm is character, and there is a kind of baptized greed for this gold. While we may wax and wane on whether we are willing to pay the price for it, it is an inherent desire in every true follower of Christ. Paul expresses this holy greed in the book of Philippians, chapter 3:

> Not that I have already obtained it, or have already become perfect, but I press on in order that I may lay hold of that for which I was laid hold of by Christ Jesus. Brethren, I do not regard my-

self as having laid hold of it yet; but one thing I do; forgetting what lies behind and reaching forward to what lies ahead I press on toward the goal for the prize of the upward call of God in Christ Jesus. (vv. 12–14)

Paul was passionate to know Christ, to become like Christ, and to obey Christ. But he recognized that he could only know Him by living the kind of life He lived, a life that included trials.

Impact on Others

You might be surprised to learn that you are the only commercial of Jesus Christ that most people will ever see. As a follower of Christ, you represent Him in your attitude, conduct, and speech at work.

Your co-workers can't see Jesus' face, but they can see yours. They likely won't feel His compassion, but they will feel yours. They can't see His response to suffering, injustice, difficult people, stress, but they will see yours and mine. But who is adequate for this? No one fully.

Even so, God has seen fit to use the likes of us to be His ambassadors (2 Corinthians 5:20), to be beacons of light in the midst of a crooked and perverse generation (Philippians 2:14–15) and limited but real reflections of who He is.

FOUR THINGS A GOOD STUDENT MUST DO

We all need character training, both building and house cleaning. As with all those He has used before us, He has to remove self-centeredness, independence, worldliness, hatred, anger, and bitterness. He wants to build patience, love, self-discipline, kindness, justice, wisdom. This is no small task. It takes hard refining to produce these results. But after God has done His work, He will use us to influence others.

Take Notice

First of all, you must realize and accept that God's purpose for you is higher than your comfort and convenience. For many, God is simply a divine waiter who exists to meet their every wish. They see God as promising to help them obtain wealth, health,

---

**"We must learn to accept pain
as our friend."**

---

and physical comfort. C. S. Lewis explains.

> What we want is not so much a Father in Heaven, as a grandfather in Heaven—a senile benevolence who as they say, "liked to see young people enjoying themselves," and whose plan for the universe was simply that it might be truly said at the end of each day, "a good time was had by all." (*The Problem of Pain*, Macmillan, New York, NY, 1962, 40)

Instead, God is more committed to making you like His Son. Unless and until we accept this goal, we will find Him to be very frustratingly confusing. We will also find that a low voltage anger toward Him saps us of all enjoyment of being in His presence, of worship, and of communing with Him.

Take Heart

Second, we must learn to accept pain as our friend. I know this sounds ridiculous! But pain appears to be God's mechanism for guiding us and keeping us from worse consequences. It hurts to touch a hot stove, but better that than leaving your hand there for a few minutes. Pain can also be like an oil light on the dashboard to warn us of a deeper problem. When that warning light comes on, the engine manual tells you to pull over and see what is going on. If you don't, five thousand moving parts in your engine may soon become one solid molten unmovable mass. C. S. Lewis made this brilliant observation: "God whispers to us in our pleasures, speaks to us in our conscience, but shouts in our pains: it is

His megaphone to rouse a deaf world." (*The Problem of Pain*, Macmillan, New York, NY, 1962, 93)

Pain can come to us just living in a fallen world where evil is still permitted to take place. But never is it without purpose. It is always possible to gain a lot from difficulty.

We often need a megaphone message from God to get us to listen.

Take Time

Third, to learn well in the schoolhouse God has given, we must reserve time to reflect on what is going on in our world and what God is teaching us. Deep and meaningful lessons are simply not doled out to the casual passerby. You will need to dedicate time to think and pray and reflect on His Word if you hope to learn well from Him (Proverbs 2). You will need the humility to look long and hard at impurities in your character, to admit them to yourself and to God.

I recommend that you keep a diary of lessons learned from work and life situations. This has proved invaluable to me personally. When I write something I feel God is teaching me in the "Lessons Learned" section of my Day-Timer, I know I will forget it soon unless I review. I don't mind getting a deeper knowledge of some previous lessons, but I don't want to learn the same lessons in the same way. Writing them down can be an invaluable way to remember what God is showing you and to learn from your past experiences.

Take Charge!

Finally, we need to do our part if we are to learn from what God sends our way.

God will not give you more pain than you and He can handle together (1 Corinthians 10:13). His goal for you is good and gentle. He loves you deeply and as a loving Father will only do what is best. But while He is there to help you, you must take charge of your own growth. You must take steps and trust God for help.

Don't accept the role of a passive victim. Take charge of your response and learn all you can from the experience.

There are some tremendous benefits to being a good learner

"We must reserve time to reflect on what is going on in our world and what God is teaching us."

---

in the school of Christlikeness.

In chapter 1 we saw that to have a good attitude you have to pursue character change and that it is not helpful to wallow in self-pity, simply wishing that our circumstances would change. In this chapter, I have suggested that we must recognize that at work we are in a schoolhouse designed by God and that we must orient ourselves to learn His lessons. However, the benefits of being a good student are unbelievable!

In the next chapter we will study Honoring Christ at Work 101. My personal experience with many individuals is that the root of most anxiety, stress, frustration, and conflict comes because they have not passed this course. The Scriptures can help us here: "Search me, O God, and know my heart. Try me and know my anxious thoughts. And see if there be any hurtful way in me, and lead me in the everlasting way" (Psalm 139:23–24).

REVIEW

Main Idea: If you are a good student, the workplace can be a schoolhouse where your character can be refined.

Key Points:

- God can make three important changes through the school-house of work trials.
  1. Christ is repositioned in your life
  2. Change can occur in your perception of life
  3. A chance to practice truth is offered
- Being a good learner has four benefits.
  1. inner peace
  2. intimacy with Christ
  3. imitation of Christ
  4. impact on others
- A good learner in this school must meet four requirements.
  1. take notice
  2. take heart
  3. take time
  4. take charge

STUDY OR DISCUSSION QUESTIONS

Part One
(20–30 minutes)

Read Proverbs 8:1–11a and consider the following questions. Keep in mind that in this passage wisdom is personified as a woman. Wisdom, however, is simply the practical application of God's Word to everyday life. God wants to give you such wisdom.

1. Why do you think Wisdom is portrayed as someone calling and lifting her voice?

2. Why does she stand at the top of the heights where the paths meet?

3. What are the benefits of gaining wisdom by listening to her words?

4. Do you agree with verse 11?

Part Two
(20–30 minutes)

Read Proverbs 2:1–5. This passage mentions the biblical requirements for learning Wisdom. The passage is in the form of an "If . . . then" statement. If you do certain things, then God will give you certain things. Note the "if" and "then" parts of the passage. Please restate them in your own words. See if you can identify a sequence in the verbs used in this passage.

If you . . . then you will. . . .

FOR PERSONAL APPLICATION

What character issues do you think God may want to help you with? Check the appropriate items below.

- [ ] having more integrity
- [ ] being more dependent on God
- [ ] having the right kind of ambition
- [ ] making Christ more important to you
- [ ] being more patient
- [ ] being more disciplined in your work
- [ ] learning to trust Christ to meet your needs
- [ ] being less concerned about what others think about you
- [ ] other issues

PART 2

A CHANGED ATTITUDE COMES FROM A CHANGED CHARACTER

— III

SKYDIVING WITHOUT A PARACHUTE: NOT RECOMMENDED

Vanities of vanities! All is vanity. What advantage does a man have in all his work which he does under the sun?

ECCLESIASTES 1:2–3

L arry has a small business that sells products for the home. He is a loving father and husband whose goal is to provide well for his family so that they will be happy. Recently I saw his wife when I was picking up my daughter from an evening church function. Casually, I asked how things were going. She said, "Terrible."

Apparently, Larry works day and night at the office and on weekends. The business is doing okay, but Larry has followed this work pattern since they were married. She is very frustrated. The kids, as you would expect, suffer from his absence. She feels all alone, and their good income does not offset her emotional needs that go wanting. When Larry comes home, there is strife and conflict. Since Larry can't understand why his family doesn't appreciate the sacrifice he is making on their behalf, this conflict is stalemated. Let's take a moment to analyze the problem.

Larry has some good goals and is sincere about them. He wants a happy family. He loves them. But his strategy to care for them is lopsided. Somehow he thinks that if he meets the material needs of the family, things will go well, and they will be happy. Obviously, this overlooks the fact that the bulk of his family's needs are emotional and spiritual. A nice home does little to meet these needs. While his goals are admirable, his unrealistic strategy fails to meet the needs of his family.

That wrong strategy could cost him his marriage and/or his relationship with his kids. It will bring stress, conflict, and confusion as to why the group at home grumbles instead of congratulating him on his ability to provide for them. So Larry is a case study in right goals (wanting to love his family) and wrong strategy (just meeting their material needs) that brings anger, stress, and tension.

In this chapter, we will look at how people like you and me make a similar mistake in our strategies at work. Often we experience difficulty at work because we look to work to meet needs that it was never designed to fulfill. Often we have some right goals or dreams, but we use work improperly to achieve them.

THREE DREAMS WE ALL HAVE

So why do most people go to work? What do they hope to gain? I believe that God has given man three primary drives that mostly find expression at work.

The first of these is the *desire for creative fulfillment*. Man was built to be a co-worker with God and to carry out the work of creation which God began and continues today. Man was created as a worker in the image of God. Thus all men and women find joy in using the strength He has given us to create something of value. It is fulfilling for the engineer to build a bridge that lasts. It is satisfying for a cabinetmaker to make beautiful cabinets.

When Gary Powers was shot down over Russia, he was confined to a political prison. Because of his "political crimes" he was sentenced not to do any work because the Soviets thought it to be a greater punishment to do no work than to be sent to the rock pile. When he was released, he said they were right. You see, God intended man to work for Him and to be creative six days of the week.

The second desire God has placed in man is the *desire for personal significance.* We all want to do something important and to be important people. We want to be needed for something important and to have worth in our own eyes and in the eyes of others. We would like to know that we matter and are making a difference in the flow of human history. We would like to know that the world is somehow a better place because of us.

Because this desire is so strong, we fear insignificance.

Our third desire is for satisfying *relationships.* We all want:

- affection
- attention
- appreciation
- acceptance

from others. We want to feel wanted. In sum, we want loyal love from others. Because our desire for these responses is so strong, we fear rejection and disapproval of others.

These deep desires are likely more a part of what drives you every day than you know. None of these desires are bad; in fact they are all very good and are God given. They are part of what makes you different from the animals, whose only goal is survival. The problem arises, however, in our strategy to meet these needs. (For a very helpful discussion of this, see Lawrence J. Crabb's *Understanding People,* Zondervan, Grand Rapids, MI, 1982.)

Tragically, man seeks to meet these needs through his own efforts and fails to rely on God.

When I was growing up, my family had a French poodle that we pampered and loved. Every day when I came home from school the dog got all excited to see me; he knew I was generous with something he was addicted to—Milkbone dog biscuits. He never got enough of these crunchy delights. Usually I went to the cabinet, and he would jump all over me while I pulled out the box. I would grab a biscuit and hold it up about shoulder height, while he jumped three feet into the air, biting the biscuit and not my hand. Then he would go to his corner to enjoy it. Within a few minutes he always came back to me, tail wagging for more. I would go into the box and hold up the next morsel about five feet high and the dog would jump with all his might to get his goal. On the third try, however, I'd hold the biscuit up over my head and he'd respond to the impossible goal by biting my foot!

Just like the dog, people are addicted to "ego biscuits"—the promotion at work, the appreciation of the boss, the applause of others. An ego biscuit is some mark of recognition for what we do that brings a momentary feeling of value. Adults, of course, acquire these ego biscuits primarily at work—from career achievement and financial success.

Often we strive to jump pretty high to get them. We worry that we won't get them and become angry if someone else blocks us from them. Once we do get them, we feel that we need more.

Our culture tells you that to meet this need for personal significance, you must do well in your career. After all, what do you call an alcoholic, who is on his third marriage, who has kids on drugs, who is selfish and egotistical, and who is the president of a Fortune 500 company? A success! Ego goals are man's attempt to fulfill his needs for creative expression, significance, and relationships without God.

But trying to fulfill your dreams without God is like skydiving without a parachute. If you do it, you are going to get hurt.

Let me suggest three specific ego strategies that people pursue to fulfill their dreams, why they fail, and the impact they have on the individual.

IF ONLY I CAN BECOME A COMPETITIVE PERSON

Many people think that if they can do better than most of their peers, they will feel significant and be appreciated by others. These people can only evaluate their worth by comparison. The worst insult they can give to a competitor is to say that he is "average."

The Strategy

A salesperson, for example, may strive to be the top salesperson in the company for this reason. Athletes want to be on the all-star team. Business people want to have the most profitable and largest company.

"Trying to fulfill your dreams without God is like skydiving without a parachute. If you do it, you are going to get hurt."

Competitors come to ten-year reunions for the purpose of favorable comparison with their peers. Their strategy to achieve personal worth and significance is to stand out from the pack and be a "winner."

Pamela Pettler articulates this thesis in a brilliantly written book, *Joy of Stress*. She writes:

> One day late in 1969 in the research library of the University of California at Berkeley, a young man went berserk. He ran through the library, shouting hysterically at his astonished fellow students, "Stop! Stop! You're getting ahead of me!"
>
> He was arrested. But what was his crime really? *Being in the wrong decade.* As we all know, the sixties era, and its childish preoccupation with peace, good sex and battered VW buses, was little more than a black mark, a shameful demerit in the History of Stress.
>
> Now, of course, in the stress-filled eighties, this concept of "getting ahead of me" has regained its rightful importance. In fact, it is one of the basic precepts of stress.
>
> Simply stated, *people are getting ahead of you.* All the time.
>
> While you're at your desk, people at the gym are getting ahead of you.

While you're at the gym, your co-workers are getting ahead of you.

If a friend gets a promotion at work, he has gotten ahead of you.

If a colleague reads a book you haven't read, he has gotten ahead of you.

The entire U.S. swim team has gotten ahead of you.

The beauty of this concept is that it can be applied across the board, anywhere, anytime.

On the road? Drivers of more expensive cars have gotten ahead of you.

Watching TV? All the writers, actors, and technical crews have gotten ahead of you.

At Marine World? All the dolphins have gotten ahead of you.

Always judge yourself, and your intrinsic moral worth, in terms of specific achievements as compared to others.

The last statement says it all. Competitors jump for competitive ego biscuits. They define their sense of impact and importance by how well they do compared to others. They imagine that they will be appreciated and loved by others for their achievement.

The Error in This Strategy

There is nothing wrong or unhealthy about being the best salesperson in the company. What is faulty thinking, however, is the mirage set up by accomplishing this goal. It simply will not deliver what is promised. Screwdrivers are useful tools, but not for eye surgery. Likewise, competition is okay, but it is not an effective tool to establish your sense of self-worth.

First of all, no matter how competitive you are, someone is always better than you. Suppose your goal is to become the president of a company doing $15 million in sales and you achieve it. There are many companies with presidents who do ten or a hundred times that in sales! If you want to be the best secretary in your law firm, and you achieve this, there are other firms to compete with. The point is that you cannot earn personal significance this way.

Secondly, if you achieve a goal, the applause does not last very long. Even if you water the eyes of your friends with your accomplishment, they don't stay impressed long. You must go out and win again. But at some point you will realize that if you have to perform to win their respect, you are not really loved or accepted for who you are as a person. Many competitors eventually become very lonely. Inevitably the attention they receive from good performance eventually fades away, and the crowd applauds someone else.

Third, the creative expression that God has given finds little fulfillment in a competitor. You see, the competitor is by nature pretty self-absorbed and self-centered. Since God built us to live on the higher ground of service, the competitor knows little of the real joy that comes from serving others.

Impact of This Strategy on You

If your strategy is to achieve personal significance from being competitive, anything that blocks you from reaching your competitive objective will make you angry.

When I was a pilot in the Air Force, we had regular check rides to evaluate our proficiency. These check rides were pretty important to our careers, and all of us did as well as we could. After one of my check rides, I came out of the parachute room where I left all my flight gear and went into the squadron. Waiting for me in the hall was Mike, a peer of mine who had taken

---

"Blocked ego goals cause anger."

---

his check ride earlier that day. Mike had done very well and scored an eighty-nine out of a possible one hundred points. Quite proud of his score, he rushed to meet me to find out how I did so he could impress me with how well he did. When he asked, I just said I did okay. But he pressed me for the score. Reluctantly, I told him I got a ninety-four. His faced turned red, and he threw his arms in the air, turned away, and screamed. He was hot. Why? Because my score blocked his goal to achieve significance. *Blocked ego goals cause anger.*

This faulty strategy has a second impact on people. Until the goal is reached, many things threaten its accomplishment. For example, a lawyer who competes with other lawyers for a partnership will find that many factors outside her control threaten her hope of success. The other lawyers may get easier case loads, easier judges, easier opposing counsel. She may face a more difficult jury. Her legal assistant may not be as good. All these complications interfere with her reaching her goal. Ultimately, she may reason that they stand in the way of her worth as a person. Thus

---

"Threatened ego goals produce stress."

---

they produce stress, often enormous stress. *Threatened ego goals produce stress.*

Bob's situation illustrates how blocked and threatened goals create problems.

Bob was recruited out of college for a fast-track management training program for a large company. Twenty-five people were selected for this program.

He was excited about his work and felt important because he was selected. At the five-year point, however, when all but two of the original twenty-five people had been promoted, Bob had not been. He was hurt and angry. To him it seemed dreadfully unfair because he had better skills than some of those who were promoted. But he hung in there.

Three years later he got the promotion but was clearly way behind his peers. By the time he turned thirty he was at the bottom of the group.

As Bob became more and more frustrated at work, he began to pour more time and emotional energy into his church where he was thought of as one of the most "faithful." He became an elder and referred regularly to the "management" role elders

---

"Accomplished ego goals leave you unsatisfied."

---

must play. While his wife was glad to see his involvement, she also noticed that Bob was gone a lot to church functions. He also developed a habit of staying up late at night. She was afraid to ask what he did during this time, but she knew that the TV was on and she always found several empty beer bottles in the morning trash.

Bob, as you can see, was really hurting. When his ego goals were threatened and blocked, he looked to church work to fill the void and alcohol to soothe the pain. His problem was that he was asking more of his work than it could deliver. Bob was disillusioned, depressed because he was trying to meet his needs through a wrong strategy. He was trying to find his self-worth and acceptance by winning at competition on the job. Eventually he found emptiness in church work because his motives were wrong.

Finally, this strategy leaves you somewhat empty when you accomplish your competitive objective. You cannot feel totally fulfilled, personally significant, or completely loved by others from this kind of accomplishment. People who dream of winning can at least enjoy the illusion. But like children who first discover what a mirage is, these people find a profound disappointment that getting to the top is not all it was cracked up to be. They usually then either pursue another mirage or become cynical. *Accomplished ego goals leave you unsatisfied.*

Competing to win approval is a strategy that leads to a dead end. It, too, is like skydiving without a parachute. If you do it, you are going to get hurt.

IF ONLY I CAN BE COMPETENT

A similar faulty strategy is working to gain significance through professional competence.

The Strategy

Many people think that if only they can prove professional competence to others, then they will feel significant and will be deeply appreciated.

People who follow this strategy usually set some rather high goals for themselves. While they, too, are concerned about being competitive, they focus on specific achievements. They want to achieve their own goals, rather than impress others.

This could involve the objective of getting a master's degree or doctorate. It could involve reaching a certain rank in military or government service. It might involve getting professional recognition.

Again, none of these accomplishments is bad in itself. But this strategy to establish self-worth or feel fulfilled is just as dead-ended as the competitive strategy. Let's take a closer look at why.

The Error in This Strategy

First of all, you will find that the finish line moves in the race for competence.

I was in a bike race once a few years ago. The stated length of the route was fifty miles. But the highway department rerouted the course the night before the race, thus, adding twelve miles to the overall distance. The race organizers did not get the word out to all the participants, including me. Well, I set my goal—and my odometer—to finish at the fifty-mile point. I pushed it as hard as I could and was totally exhausted at fifty miles. But at fifty-three miles there was no finish line in sight. At fifty-five miles I stopped, psychologically and physically beaten. The finish line moved. I was really upset. (Yes, you guessed it. I am a competitor; when my goal was blocked, I was angry.)

Something similar happens when you pursue a competency goal. You think you're about to cross the finish line and suddenly it moves. Suddenly, just having a college degree is not enough. Just having a master's is not enough. You need a doctorate—and, of course, not just any doctorate will do.

Again as with the competitive strategy, the applause doesn't last long. *The finish line moves.*

The Impact of This Strategy on You

The basic rules follow. Blocked goals bring anger, threatened goals bring stress, and achieved goals are not all they are cracked up to be.

Again, this strategy will leave you empty. You were born to live for more than selfish and egotistical goals.

IF ONLY I CAN BE A CONSUMER OF LUXURY ITEMS

Competing and pursuing competency are dead-end strategies for meeting your needs for significance and loyal relationships. So is the consumption of luxury items.

The Strategy

Someone once said, "We buy what we don't need to impress people we don't know with money we don't have."

We all have a touch of this syndrome. We have come to believe that if we have a nice home, drive an impressive car, and have enough money to do whatever we want, we will feel personally significant, loved by others, and fulfilled in what we do. The trouble is that the only people who believe this are the people who don't have it.

The Error in This Strategy

This one is not hard to refute. No matter what you have, you can always want more. No matter how nice your house, clothes, car, there are nicer ones. In fact, the more you desire money, the less content you will be with what you have, according to Ecclesiastes 5:10: "Whoever loves money will never be satisfied with money."

Now it is not hard to see that if your personal significance depends on the acquisition of material things, you are building a house on sand.

Regularly, when I speak on this topic, I poll groups from a wide range of backgrounds—rich and poor, religious and irreligious. I ask them, "If you could make twice as much income as you do today, do you think you would be fundamentally happier and more fulfilled?" Almost everyone smiles uneasily and says, yes! Then I ask how many today are making significantly more today than they did five years ago. Of those who raise their hands I ask, "Are you fundamentally happier? Do you have more inner peace and more of a sense of personal significance because of your increase?" Almost without exception, no one says yes.

The Impact of This Strategy on You

Blocked goals bring anger.

Kathy had been eyeing the rings that her friends wore with envy. She had hoped that she could have one herself and felt a little insignificant because she had only a wedding band. She dropped several hints to her husband, but he rightly concluded that they couldn't afford it. She became a little discouraged but began to pray that either she or her husband would get a raise. Her husband came home after his yearly employee evaluation saying that he would not get a raise this year. She became furious. Her goal was blocked.

Threatened goals bring stress.

Jake was a salesman. He had been working for six months on an account in Cleveland. If the company placed the large order under consideration, he would make a very large commission and his family would be able to buy a new home. The decision would be made in one week by the president of the company. Jake was having trouble sleeping. He was worried about what factors might bring about a negative decision. So much seemed to be riding on this sale that he found it hard to relax. He wondered if he should mentally assume that it wouldn't come in so as not to be disappointed. Then his wife asked if they could go looking at new homes. As they went with the realtor, he felt so much

---

"If your personal significance depends on the acquisition of material things, you are building a house on sand."

---

stress he nearly choked. What would happen to them if the sale did not come through. It seemed that his family's happiness, his role as a provider, and his sense of worth were at stake. The threat of a negative decision by the Cleveland company was very real and produced a lot of stress.

Accomplished consumption goals do not bring you all that you think.

When my wife and I were in graduate school, our living room couch had a bad tear in it. We were pretty disgusted with it. When we had guests over, foam rubber oozed between the legs of whoever sat on the spot with the tear. It was so embarrassing. We longed for the day when we could buy a new couch. When the time finally came, we were so excited. We replaced it and made two unsuccessful efforts to give the old one away.

We were so happy with our new couch, for about an hour. Then the pleasure seemed to evaporate. When one of the kids spilled chili on it, we began to dream of something else. The thrill was gone, as they say.

Earning a raise, making the sale, and getting new furniture are fine goals. But God does not want you to be addicted to them. He wants to meet your three basic needs through a relationship with Him. When you find yourself angry or stressed, it is good to ask yourself why? Be careful, too, when you find yourself thinking, "Boy, when we can afford _____, then we will really be happy." Rarely is this the case. Just think of your most recent purchase. How much true joy and significance does it bring you?

WHY PURSUING EGO GOALS BRINGS ANGER, STRESS, AND ULTIMATELY EMPTINESS

Think of what is at stake. If you are trying to prove your worth as a person, you have a lot to worry about. After all, think of how painful it would be to be "insignificant." Suppose people laughed at you or simply underestimated you. The fear of rejection and the fear of insignificance are critical fears that you will seek to allay. Anyone or anything that gets in your way will be a major threat. After all, the workplace provides regular threats to ego goals.

I take a magazine called *Success*. It often chronicles the story of successful business people and how they achieved success on their own. I am convinced the angels in heaven fall down laughing at the thought that people make it on their own. The fact is that most of the factors that make a person successful are beyond our control.

A farmer is vulnerable to drought, to insects, to farm subsidies, to national and international market conditions. Surely he must work hard, but most of the factors of success are out of his control. Farmers are often humble people who understand this, but all of us are just as vulnerable, even if we think we are really in control.

Think of the factors of your career that are out of your control: your health, interest rates, market conditions, legislation, management, labor, weather. The list goes on and on. Now if you have your worth as a person on the line, you are going to go from one threat to another—always stressed out!

Another issue at work is that other people will never appreciate you fully. In fact, it's reasonable to expect that others are self-absorbed—looking after their own interests and mostly impressed with themselves. You are there for their benefit. If you sail into work each day expecting your value as a person to be buoyed by the flow of admiring comments from co-workers, you will be in trouble. If you succeed, people will be envious; if you fail, some will be delighted. You can't base your worth on impressing others.

I live in Washington, D.C., a city that illustrates how impossible it is to really impress people. Recently a presidential candidate who lost a bid for his party's nomination was appointed to a cabinet post. The press and the hushed remarks at parties suggest that he is a loser. Can you believe it? However ridiculous it is, it

---

"People are mostly impressed with themselves, and their memories of others' success are short."

---

portrays the futility of basing your worth on impressing others. *People are mostly impressed with themselves, and their memories of others' success are short.*

Can you remember who won the Superbowl in 1984? Who was King of England in 1532? The psalmist says it best I think.

> As for man, his days are like grass;
> As the flower of the field flourishes.
> When the wind has passed over it, it is no more;
> And its place acknowledges it no longer.
> (Psalm 103:15–16)

Finally, you need to know that "getting to the top of the ladder is not all it's supposed to be." In fact, many successful people have confided in me that they would trade places in a moment with a poor, happy person.

C'MON! WHAT'S WRONG WITH CAREER ACHIEVEMENT?

Absolutely nothing! My hope is that God would give you great success. My point is simply this: Your dreams of creative fulfillment, of significance, and for loyal relationships cannot ultimately be realized through the pursuit of ego strategies in the workplace. If you try, you will be angered at the frequent recurrence of blocked goals; you will be very stressed by the factors all around you that are out of your control; and you will feel empty, perhaps becoming a self-centered person.

Success can be a gift from God, but you are never to be addicted to it. God designed you for a more noble existence than simply jumping for ego biscuits. He also wants you to have a sense of significance totally independent from the ups and downs of your job. He wants you to do work that is fulfilling and appreciated. *He wants you to have a radically different view of why you go to work and how you assess the results of your labor.*

The next two chapters will address these perspectives.

So far you have seen what work is like without God in the picture. It is a treadmill. It is a dog's existence. It is vain, futile. It is skydiving without a parachute.

Only in Christ will you find true and lasting significance. Only the work you do for Christ can give real meaning and a sense of impact. Only in your relationship with Christ can you be ultimately respected, appreciated, loved, and rewarded for what you do all day.

The goal of working for Christ can never be blocked, never be threatened, and the accomplishment of the goal will leave you with a smile.

REVIEW

> **Main Idea: Trying to fulfill your dreams for fulfillment, significance, and relationships through ego strategies is like skydiving without a parachute.**

Key Points:

- Man was created with the desire for creative fulfillment, significance, and loyal relationships.
- Man tries to fulfill these dreams through ego strategies of:
  1. competition
  2. competency
  3. consumption of luxury materials
- These strategies cannot satisfy man's deepest longings; they lead to anger, stress, and emptiness.
- Ego strategies do not work for several reasons.
  1. Most factors of success are out of your control.
  2. People are impossible to impress.
  3. Pursuing ego goals leaves you self-centered and poor in character and relationships.
  4. God has made you to live for a higher purpose than jumping for ego biscuits.
- Only in Christ can your needs be met.
- God wants to give you a radically different view of why you go to work and how you assess the results of your labor.

STUDY OR DISCUSSION QUESTIONS

Part One
(20–30 minutes)

Instructions: Take the following quiz, and answer the subsequent questions either *Y* for yes or *N* for no.

- ☐ I am bothered when a peer of mine gets a promotion ahead of me.

- ☐ I am somewhat embarrassed by my educational achievements.

- ☐ I am bothered by my physical appearance due to a lack of diet and exercise.

☐ I frequently wonder what people think after meeting me.

☐ I am in turmoil for days after I have been corrected by a superior.

☐ I feel depressed when I hear someone sing the praise of another co-worker.

☐ I have special skills that my superiors do not appreciate.

☐ I have to admit that I tend to brag about myself, even subtly, when in conversation.

☐ I have few close friends with whom I could share an intimate problem.

☐ I frequently daydream about making an unusual contribution in my career.

☐ My associates would say that I am ambitious.

☐ My associates would say that I tend to be self-absorbed and not very thoughtful of others.

☐ My anger level tends to be high as I deal with work problems. The thing that really made me mad recently was . . .

☐ My stress level is usually pretty high.

☐ I tend to feel a little embarrassed when I have people over to my home. I wish it were bigger.

☐ I think about my image with others a lot.

☐ I think a lot about buying a new car.

Questions:

1. Which questions above relate to competitive strategies?

2. Which questions relate to competency strategies?

3. Which questions relate to consumption strategies?

4. Which of the ego strategies are you most susceptible to?

5. As a result of taking this quiz, what did you learn about yourself?

Part Two
(20–30 minutes)

1. Read Daniel 4:1–37. What was the lesson King Nebuchadnezzar was supposed to learn, that having not learned he was sent on a camping trip?

2. What lesson could you take from this study?

3. What are some practical ways you could seek God's glory?

— IV

INTRODUCING YOUR NEW BOSS

Slaves, be obedient to those who are your masters according to the flesh, with fear and trembling, in the sincerity of your heart as to Christ; not by way of eyeservice as menpleasers, but as slaves of Christ, doing the will of God from the heart.

With good will render service as to the Lord and not to men, knowing that whatever good thing each one does, this he will receive back from the Lord whether slave or free.

EPHESIANS 6:5–8

This is radical! So far we have identified that motivation for work commonly centers on ego goals. Being competitive, being competent, and being a consumer of luxury items are common ego strategies to feel important and to win the loyal love of others. But God has called you to something much higher than simply jumping for ego biscuits. He actually invites you to work for Him, to see your career in a radically different and enormously freeing way! He wants you to see Him as your real boss.

This simple concept is the most important building block in a new attitude about your work. No matter how difficult, how stressful, or how boring your job, seeing your work the way God does and doing it for Him can give you:

- more joy
- more self-respect
- more of a sense of significance
- more freedom from needing to impress others

To begin to get a new perspective on your work you need to see work through the eyes of God Himself. His view can be summarized in three ideas:

1. Your work is an extension of God's work.

2. Your work is a service to others.

3. Your real boss is Jesus Christ.

Let's unpack each of these ideas to help you gain a radically new perspective on what you do all day.

YOUR WORK SHOULD BE SEEN AS AN EXTENSION OF GOD'S WORK

According to Scripture you go to work for the same reason you go to church, to worship and serve Jesus Christ. Two principles are foundational to this thought.

God Is a Worker

New as this idea may seem to you, God Himself is a worker who is as invested in His work as you are in yours. In the opening chapter of the Bible we are introduced to a God who works. In Genesis 1, we see God making the "expanse" (v. 7), making "the two great lights" (v. 16), creating "the great sea monsters and every living creature that moves" (v. 21). Throughout this wonderful introduction to God, we see Him as an active worker. In fact, chapter 2 verse 2 says that "by the seventh day God completed *his work* which He had done" (emphasis added). The Hebrew word for "work" here is the same word used for man's work in Exodus 20, when we are commanded, "six days you shall labor and do all your *work*" (v. 9, emphasis added). You see, like you, God is a worker.

Not only did God create the world, but He is actively in-

"[God] actually invites you to work for Him . . . ! He wants you to see Him as your real boss."

---

volved in the affairs of everyday life. Because of His love for man, He "works" to meet the physical, emotional, and spiritual needs of man. His work is both perfect and wonderful.

In the Psalms He is praised for His continued work in creation:

> Great are the works of the LORD;
> They are studied by all who delight in them.
> Splendid and majestic is His work;
> And His righteousness endures forever.
> He has made His wonders to be remembered;
> The LORD is gracious and compassionate.
> He has given food to those who fear Him;
> He will remember His covenant forever.
> He has made known to His people the power of
> His works.
>
> (Psalm 111:2–6a)

His work involves giving you food and clothing and meeting a wide range of needs. His work involves health care, farming, and government. He is a worker who meets a broad range of physical, emotional, and spiritual needs. Consider another passage from Psalms:

> He causes the grass to grow for cattle,
> And vegetation for the labor of man
> So that he may bring forth food from the earth.
>
> (Psalm 104:14)

You see, God is a worker. The fact that you eat daily is one clear way you can see His work.

You Are His Co-worker

While God created the world and is still active in it, He has chosen man to be His junior partner to carry out His work.

Let's go back to Genesis 1. In the first twenty-five verses of this chapter, God is revealed as a worker. In verse 26, we read, "Then God said, 'Let Us make man in Our image, according to Our likeness; and let them rule over the fish of the sea and over the birds of the sky and over the cattle and over all the earth and over every creeping thing that creeps on the earth.'"

Maybe you work with one of these creeps! (Just kidding.)

Seriously, you were created by God to be His junior partner. You are to carry out His work in the world. As Adam was put in the Garden of Eden to "cultivate it and keep it," so you have been given work in His creation to cultivate it and keep it.

Think of your breakfast this morning. Undoubtedly you thanked God for your cereal or eggs, and rightfully so. But how did God actually get that food to you? He used the grocer, the boy who stocked the shelves, the truck driver who delivered the food to the store, and even the maker of the pallets upon which the food rested in the truck. He used a complex web of people to meet your need. He could have food fall from the sky, but His way is to use man to carry out His work.

As you can see, this view lends tremendous dignity to what you do all day. If you are a nurse, you help to meet the health needs of people He loves. If you are an engineer building bridges, you help to meet the transportation needs of your city. Your work is as important as the work of any pastor or missionary. You are meeting needs He wants met for people He deeply loves and cares about.

But unlike those who only work for their own ego gratification, you have a higher calling. Work, as God intended it, is a gift from the Lord to bring glory to Him. It is a gift, a high honor that you have your job. The psalmist says,

When I consider Thy heavens, the work of Thy fingers,
The moon and the stars, which Thou hast ordained;
What is man that Thou dost take thought of Him?
And the son of man that Thou dost care for him?
Yet Thou hast made him a little lower than God,
And dost crown him with glory and majesty!
Thou dost make him to rule over the works
    of Thy hands.

                      (Psalm 8:3–6)

But the point of this high calling is to bring glory to God, not ourselves. Thus your focus and perspective at work should be to bring glory to God by the way you do your work. Your integrity, the excellence you bring to your job, your ambition, and the quality of your peer relationships can all reflect the glory of the Savior.

When I entered the Air Force Academy, I was enrolled in a difficult training program to prepare to be a leader in the service of my country. We were told it was an honor to wear the uniform, to serve, and maybe to die for the freedoms we enjoy and

---

"Work, as God intended it, is a gift from the Lord to bring glory to Him."

---

hold dear. The uniform is a symbol of the high ideals of duty, honor, and freedom. There is a whole code of ethics for what you can and cannot do in uniform.

As a follower of Christ in your daily work, you are always in uniform. You are never to forget the high honor of being in His service. You are to bring credit to the One who enlisted you. In sum, you are to live a life so unique and so distinctive that your co-workers will wonder why.

You are the only commercial most people will ever see of what Jesus Christ is like. However dim the light is, they should find in you a work style that brings credit to the Savior. Colossians 3:23–24 says this: "Whatever you do, do your work heart-ily, as for the Lord rather than for men. . . . It is the Lord Christ whom you serve."

But there is another dimension to your work.

YOUR WORK SHOULD BE A SERVICE TO OTHERS

As I mentioned earlier, your work is to be an extension of God's work for others. It is an extension of His love. It involves meeting needs He cares about. So a Christlike approach to work involves caring about the needs of others. If you are a receptionist, you should care for the people who call your company. You are there as a servant to them and to those in your company. If you are a salesman, you are to care for the needs of your clients and prospects. In short, you are to love people through your work.

In Matthew 22 Jesus responds to a lawyer's question.

"Teacher, which is the great commandment in the Law?"
And He said to him, "'You shall love the Lord your God with all your heart, and with all your soul, and with all your mind.' This is the great and foremost commandment. And the second is like it. 'You shall love your neighbor as yourself.'" (vv. 36–39)

Martin Luther said a cobbler loves his neighbor by making good shoes. This is good theology.

It is true that you work for a paycheck to meet your needs. But you are also called to love your neighbor in and through your work.

Your hands are the hands of Jesus Christ that meet the needs of others. This implies that you see yourself as a servant, that you really care about helping others. As a car salesman, you find out what people really need and do your best to find the right product to meet their need. As an executive, you care deeply about your customers and employees. This new mindset is a servant orientation, not a self-centered one.

Being a servant also means that you do your work with excellence, enthusiasm, and ethics.

Have you ever flown on a commercial airliner? If you have, you know that takeoff is a little tense for passengers. It's even more tense in the cockpit. You see, on every takeoff there is a chance for an engine to fail. Pilots calculate a speed called v-one. If an engine is lost under this speed, they are supposed to stop the aircraft. Above that speed, they are supposed to continue takeoff even with only one engine operating. On takeoff roll, the

---

"Your hands are the hands of Jesus Christ that meet the needs of others."

---

aircraft accelerates very fast, so the pilot must pay close attention to what is happening in the cockpit. You would not want him to be reading the latest issue of *Time* or *Newsweek* during takeoff. You depend on him or her to do the work with excellence. So people depend on you. A servant does excellent work.

Have you ever been to a barber or hair stylist on Friday afternoon? Imagine going for your appointment at five in the evening. You ask her how her day is going, and she says to you, "Terrible. It's going terrible. I hate this job. I'm so tired. I can't wait to finish up with you so I can go home."

What would you be thinking? You probably would be wondering if you'll walk out of there looking like Mr. T!

A servant does his or her work with enthusiasm because a servant cares.

Finally, imagine your son or daughter becoming so sick you take the child to the doctor. The doctor recommends surgery. How important to you is it that he tells the truth about the actual need for the surgery? Probably pretty important!

So, too, people depend on you to tell the truth in your job and to have integrity. A servant does his or her work with ethics.

Perhaps this is a start at a servant's manifesto.

- I will care about the needs of my company's clients/customers.
- I will focus my attention on doing a good job for the people who depend on me.
- I will be more concerned about helping others than getting credit for myself.
- I will do my work with excellence, enthusiasm, and ethics.

Undoubtedly, you are wondering if anyone will notice or appreciate this perspective. Maybe yes, maybe no. But for you, the personal advantages to this attitude are tremendous.

First, you will be happier. You see, God built you to glorify Him and serve others. When you do this, you can have a joy that exists above your circumstances. There is something entirely unsatisfying about being self-absorbed or egotistical. Relationships tend to be shallow and lack intimacy when we are focusing on our own glory or our needs. A Christian will feel this emptiness more than one outside of Christ because he knows better. Down deep we know that even Christ Himself did not come to seek His own glory but the glory of His Father. After all, He said, "If I glorify Myself, My glory is nothing" (John 8:54).

Second, you can have more self-respect by living on higher ground than by simply being selfish.

During my first year at the U.S.A.F. Academy, we had a grueling survival program. We were let off in the mountains of Colorado to travel for about five days with little more than a candy bar and some water. The terrain was rugged; it was cold at night and hot during the day, and it rained nearly every afternoon. But the hardest part of the survival program was the lack of food. At the end of the week, we debriefed the program *en masse* in the mountains after all of my classmates were collected. We looked pretty grungy and were famished. After the briefing, a steak dinner was served.

As you might imagine, there was a stampede. Men at the head of the line took three or four steaks, even though the rule was one per person. By the time those of us at the end of the line got to the tables, there were only some baked potatoes left. Can you imagine how those who "got theirs" must have felt later? Even though their bellies were full, do you suppose their selfishness brought them much self-respect?

"The Lord is your real boss and you go to work each day to do His work and to do it His way."

Servants do not always get as much steak as self-centered people do. But they do have a lot more self-respect. They are sustained by the fact that they are pleasing God.

Jesus Himself said, "My food is to do the will of Him who sent Me, and to accomplish His work" (John 4:34).

Having a Christlike servant attitude at work is simply a better way to live and work.

YOUR REAL BOSS SHOULD BE JESUS CHRIST

Perhaps the best way to summarize all that has been said is that the Lord is your real boss and you go to work each day to do His work and to do it His way. You serve Him and others. If He is your boss, three ideas follow.

You Do Your Work to Please Him, Not to Impress Others

Every year that I was a pilot in the Air Force, our squadron had an inspection. Usually, we got the word through the grapevine about two weeks before the inspection that the Inspector General was coming to review and evaluate the performance of our operation. The outcome of the inspection would determine the career status of several of our superiors.

You would be amazed at the work that was done to prepare for the evaluation! We would not have worked as hard to prepare for invasion by a foreign country! Haircuts were short, pilots sharpened their skills and read documents that they were supposed to know, and in general the entire base "got its act together."

We used to say that the two biggest lies in the Air Force were told when the Inspector General landed with his team. First, the squadron commander would salute the I.G. and say, "We're glad you're here." Then the I.G. would say, "We are here to help."

No matter what your career, you can find a similar dynamic. People often do their work to impress others and have a whole different work style when supervisors are watching. Not you. You should be different.

The follower of Christ maintains a level of excellence whether anyone is watching or not because he does his work for Christ—every day.

Consider the passage at the beginning of this chapter. According to Paul, we are to do our work "as to Christ . . . not by way of eyeservice as men-pleasers."

Two important ideas flow from this profound text.

First, we are to dedicate each day's work to Christ.

Recently in Baltimore a college basketball star died unexpectedly. The whole town grieved over the loss of a very fine young man. The team dedicated each of the next several games to his memory, and they played their hearts out. Their performance was compelling to watch. You, of course, "play the game" at your job for a higher purpose than this college team. You work for Jesus Christ and dedicate each day to Him.

Second, it is enough that Jesus is pleased with your work. There is no one to impress, and nothing to prove. Men are fickle in their appreciation. If you do a good job, you may be noticed and rewarded fairly, or as is often the case, you may not be.

But Christ *always* notices and rewards good work you do for Him. In fact, he promises that "whatever good thing each one does, this he will receive back from the Lord whether slave or free" (Ephesians 6:8).

Think of it: a perfect and just system of rewards. Sometimes God will reward you on earth with promotions or with more responsibility. But always you will be rewarded in heaven for every good work you do for Christ!

Now if most of your life is spent working, then it follows that most of your rewards in heaven will come for the work you do to honor Him!

This brings so much freedom from the need for others' approval. Depending on man for appreciation is like depending on

---

"Christ always notices and rewards good work you do for Him."

---

your eight-year-old to drive your family safely across country on vacation! Only in Christ will real glory be found. And only to Him can we look for real appreciation and approval.

Jesus Christ is the best boss you could ever have! Now, more on what it means to make Him your boss.

You Keep Him Central in Your Workday

As I travel across the country, I am encouraged that more and more Christians are seeking to make Christ a real part of their work experience each day. They have become dissatisfied with just a Sunday morning religion and either want Christ to be a major part of their lives or to quit pretending so on Sunday. They intuitively understand that to make Him their boss means making Him a central part of each workday. To do this involves daily seeking His wisdom and seeking His Face.

Seeking His wisdom. The Bible suggests that wisdom is the skill of applying God's word to everyday situations. The same Hebrew word is used for a silversmith who crafts silver ore into a beautiful vessel. It is a skill, a craft.

Making Christ Lord of your work means that you become a student in the school of His wisdom (recall chapter 2). It means you read the Bible to find out how it applies to issues you face at work. For the life of me I cannot imagine a person not taking advantage of the wealth of wisdom and encouragement the Scriptures have to offer. Too many read the Bible thinking that God only speaks to their church or family life. But there is more said about work in the Bible than about the family or money or prayer or church. Fully two-thirds of Jesus' parables have work illustrations.

Sometimes after I speak to groups, a sincere individual makes a comment that goes something like this: "I don't see why you are making such a big deal about honoring Christ at work. If you just follow a few simple principles you will be okay."

There is some truth to the comment if we see the Great Commandments as the "simple principles." However, the comment often misses the complexities of what it means to love your neighbor at work and to love Christ with all your heart. The Scriptures are filled with practical wisdom on issues like:

- conflict resolution
- stress
- balancing work and nonwork responsibilities
- impossible job demands
- dealing with injustice
- significance
- decision making and problem solving
- anger and how to deal with it
- relational skills

To make Christ Lord of your work means that you study what He says on these topics—as you are doing by reading this book. The true follower of Christ daily seeks wisdom for how to honor Him at work.

Seeking His face. Have you ever thought about what Christ's face looks like? Consider those deep, dark eyes that can look right into your soul. Imagine the scars on His face from the crown of thorns. Imagine your feeling of being in His presence! What would His expression be? At one and the same time it would be both terrifying and peaceful. It would be like being in the presence of both a lion and a lamb. You would feel His love and His devotion to you. Likely you would feel very inadequate.

If you could meet Him face to face, what would you say to Him and what would He say to you?

These are profound questions. But you should ask them daily. Psalm 105:4 says,

> Seek the LORD and His strength;
> Seek His face continually.

To seek the face of Christ daily could involve many things. But imagine yourself asking three simple questions throughout the day.

"Lord Jesus, what would *You* have me do in this situation?"

"Lord Jesus, how would *You* have me respond to this person?"

"Lord Jesus, what attitude would *You* have me maintain in this situation?"

Could you imagine how different your workday could be if these questions were frequently asked? You see, the Lord is your boss and His employees "seek His face continually."

Now, let's consider a third principle of making Christ your real boss.

You Do Not Take Too Much Responsibility Or Credit for the Results of Your Work

It is important to see that you are really just a junior partner with Him in your work.

Consider a farmer's work. He tills the soil, plants the seed, and harvests the crops. But he can't control the rain or the temperature or stop a locust invasion. In fact, most of the elements of his success are out of his control. They are in the hands of God. The farmer is just a junior partner with God in the harvest.

Consider the aspects of your success or the success of your company that are out of your control.

- interest rates
- international market conditions
- weather
- market variations
- defense cutbacks

If you think about it, a lot of factors are completely out of your control. All you are responsible for is your part. You "sow the seed"; God's responsibility is to bring the rain and sunshine. If the crops are not as large as you want, you accept the harvest with gratitude, for it comes from Him and you trust that He knows what is best for you.

On the other hand, if we get a bumper crop, we don't take the credit for it. His blessing brings our success, not the wonderful personality we bring to the table. We should never so inflate our value that we miss how much of our success depends on His blessing. Paul says, "For through the grace given to me I say to every man among you not to think more highly of himself than he ought to think; but to think so as to have sound judgment" (Romans 12:3).

You and I are just junior partners. In chapter 6 we will press this idea a little further.

Thus far you have to be struck with how radical it is to see Christ as your real boss. But perhaps you can also sense how freeing it is: no one (human that is) to impress, nothing to prove. These concepts are liberating. So far we have looked at the first of these ideas. In the next chapter, we will turn to the second idea— nothing to prove. We all want a sense of personal worth. We want to be needed and appreciated. We want to know that our lives will count for something and will make a mark. So far we have seen the futility of trying to impress men and the failure of ego goals to satisfy. But that still begs the question, how does one get that feeling we all thirst for? Next chapter!

REVIEW

> **Main Idea: Accepting Christ as your real boss can bring you more joy, self-respect, significance, and freedom.**

Key Points:

- Your work should be seen as an extension of God's work.
  1. God is a worker.
  2. You are His co-worker.
- Your work should be seen as a service to others.
  1. A servant does His work with excellence.
  2. A servant does His work with enthusiasm.
  3. A servant does His work with ethics.
- Your real boss should be Jesus Christ.
  1. You do your work to please Him, not to impress others.
  2. You keep Him central in your workday.
  3. You seek His wisdom.
  4. You seek His face.
  5. You ask: What would You have me do?
  6. You ask: How would You have me respond?
  7. You ask: What attitude would You have me maintain?
  8. You do not take too much responsibility or credit for the results of your work.

STUDY OR DISCUSSION QUESTIONS

Part One
(40–60 minutes)

Instructions: Answer the following questions from the material you have just studied. Place a *T* for true or *F* for false. If you are in a group, explain your answers.

☐ God cares mostly about "spiritual" work like that of a pastor.

☐ The "calling" of a pastor is higher than that of a carpenter.

☐ God's love for humanity pervades all areas of life including the physical and emotional needs.

☐ The only time we "really" serve the Lord is at church.

☐ The rules of the game change from Sunday to Monday.

☐ It is impossible to be a "servant" in today's world and still survive.

☐ A person who really does his work as unto the Lord will naturally have a better attitude toward the work.

☐ I believe that my integrity is my most valuable possession, and I would sacrifice my career if necessary to keep my conscience clean before God.

☐ I find it hard to remember to pray to God during my workday.

☐ I find it hard to apply the Bible and the time it was written to today's fast-paced marketplace.

The following questions ask for your opinions. Simply answer the questions or complete the sentences.

1. God has chosen people to be His co-workers because . . .

2. In your work, a person with a "servant" mindset would be perceived by others as . . .

3. What kind of eternal rewards will be offered to those who do their work with excellence, enthusiasm, and ethics?

4. How would you describe the difference between doing your work for Christ and doing it for your ego?

5. What are some specific habits you could cultivate as a result of this chapter?

Finally, study Ephesians 6:5–8. List every principle in the passage you can find. See if you find twelve ideas in the passage!

— V

RIDING THE ROLLER COASTER OF PERSONAL SIGNIFICANCE

When I consider Thy heavens, the work
of Thy fingers, the moon and the stars
which Thou hast ordained; What is man,
that Thou dost take thought of him? And
the son of man that Thou dost care for
him? Yet Thou hast made him a little
lower than God, and dost crown him
with glory and majesty!

PSALM 8:3–5

H ave you ever seen a gymnastics event on TV? Participants swing, jump, tumble, and balance precariously on a beam performing graceful complicated moves for the judges and the crowd. After their performance, the judges hold up their score based on the degree of difficulty and the technical excellence with which they performed. Contestants await that score with nervous anticipation to see if their hunches about how they did match those of the judges. If they anticipated a 9.0 and got a 9.4, they

77

are, of course, elated. If it goes the other way, the final score might seem unfair. But in either case, their gymnastics performance scores are not indicators of their personal worth or significance—or are they?

YOUR CHOICE—ONE JUDGE OR MANY?

As was mentioned in chapter 3, many take the cues for their sense of importance from other people (the judges), attempting to achieve enough in their careers to earn a 10 for the crowd around them. These people think that career competency, competitiveness, or consumption of luxury items will win respect, admiration, and loyal relationships. They are equally convinced that if they achieve poor scores, they will feel insignificant and will be criticized and rejected by others.

Our boss, our friends and neighbors, our family, our co-workers, and even people we do not know, it seems, form a sometimes silent group of judges who evaluate our achievement.

As we have already seen, however, boosting our egos through ego biscuits brings only momentary satisfaction. The blocking or threatening of our ego goals produces anger and stress. But even when ego goals are achieved, they bring only emptiness.

The question is, how can your sense of personal worth endure the ups and downs of a career and be unaffected by people's appreciation of you?

TRUE SIGNIFICANCE COMES FROM ACCEPTING GOD'S VIEW OF YOU

In the crowd around you, some will hold up a 7, some a 2, and some a 9. But the most important judge in the universe will always hold up a 10. God has a very high view of your worth, and accepting His opinion of you is the first step to a healthy self-image that can survive the bumps and bruises of a career. But you must accept His score of 10 for you by faith. In many ways it is like becoming a Christian; it is a step of faith.

Have you ever talked to a person about trusting Christ? You may have found a common frustration. The most common objection I hear from people is that they do not feel they need any help getting to heaven. They feel they already merit God's favor and don't need the Savior. If you insist that the Bible calls salvation a "gift," not a "wage," they balk. Often people feel their good deeds outweigh their bad, or they can't imagine anything they have done that might separate them from God.

When you face these objections, you go to God's Word. According to God, salvation is nothing you can take credit for (Ephesians 2:8–9). It would be like a person bragging about his wisdom and skill at picking the right family to be born into.

Salvation is a gift from God accepted by faith. In his pride man pursues good works, to earn salvation as a wage. God's way and man's way are very different. One is through faith; the other is by works. These two approaches are reviewed below.

God's Way	Man's Way
A gift from God	Earned through human effort
Accepted by faith	Belief that personal feelings are right
Belief in God's Word despite feelings	Feeling that salvation is deserved regardless of belief

Perhaps this chart will reveal the vastness of the chasm between God's way and man's.

When you came to Christ, you fundamentally decided to trust what God said—that you were a sinner in need of the Savior. On the basis of His work on the cross, you believed that you could have eternal life as a free gift.

But just as you went through this process to have eternal life, you must go through a very similar one to obtain a sense of personal significance. You must:

- recognize it as a gift from God, not something you can earn through your own efforts; it can only be a gift, not a wage.
- believe what He says about you in His Word despite your feelings to the contrary.

Let us take a look at each of these ideas in more detail.

PERSONAL SIGNIFICANCE IS GIVEN TO YOU AS A GIFT

God's intention is to give you, free of charge, a sense of personal worth that can in no way be enhanced or diluted by your performance. His view of you is much higher than you could ever have of yourself, and unless and until we accept His view of us as the score that really counts, we will be very insecure.

The very fact that you were created by God gives you inherent worth and value. You were made "in the image of God" (Genesis 1:26). This truth has profound meaning! Your place in the ladder of creation is just "a little lower than God" (Psalm 8:5).

When my wife Jan was pregnant with our first child, I went to work to build a crib. Not just any crib, though. This was to be

---

"[God] made us! He is very proud of what He has made, and He did not make a mistake."

---

a crib that would swing; it would last our son for at least two years and maybe even be something that he would use with his children. A friend of mine, when he saw this creation of mine, thought it would last him till he became a teenager. It was huge! We had to put it in the middle of the room so that it could swing. Jan was very gracious, but my friends spared no remarks in teasing me about it. When Jason finally came and we put him in it, I was so proud of what I had built. It felt good to create something so useful—even if the beauty was singularly in the eye of the beholder.

But this imperfect analogy applies to the way God sees you and me. He made us! He is very proud of what He has made, and He did not make a mistake. Psalm 8 tells us that man is the most important thing God created and that while there is feeling for all of creation, He has given man the highest position in His creative order. *Point one: God made you and is very proud of what He has made.*

Secondly, God both knows you and loves you. As I reflect on this fact, I seem to be able to accept one or the other but not both. If I think of God as a senile, benevolent person who really does not know me, then I can accept that He could love me. But if I think of His knowing me inside and out—thoughts and actions—I find it hard to imagine His love. But both are true, and His knowledge of us and His love is greater than we know. Consider again this crucial passage from the Psalms.

> O LORD, Thou hast searched me and known me.
> Thou dost know when I sit down and rise up;
> Thou dost understand my thought from afar.
> Thou dost scrutinize my path and my lying down,
> And art intimately acquainted with all my ways.
> Even before there is a word on my tongue,
> Behold, O LORD, Thou dost know it all.
> (Psalm 139:1–4)

He knows all your thoughts and your words and your actions. He is *intimately* acquainted with all your ways.

When our kids were toddlers, Jan had an amazing ability to decipher their language. Early attempts at the English language came out in Syrophonecian to most adults around them. But their mother knew them intimately and could interpret the garbled signals.

God knows you much better than a mother knows her children. He knows you, your thoughts, and your ways intimately.

This would be scary except for the fact that He deeply loves you. In the same Psalm, the writer goes on to say,

> How precious are Thy thoughts to me, O God!
> How vast is the sum of them!
> If I should count them, they would outnumber
>   the sand.
> When I awake I am still with Thee. (vv. 17–18)

In the New Testament, the Apostle Paul tells the church in Ephesus what He seeks for them in prayer. Whenever Paul does this in His letters, he is making an emphatic point. In chapter 3, he prays that they "may be able to comprehend with all the saints what is the breadth and length and height and depth and to know the love of Christ which surpasses knowledge, that you may be filled up to all the fullness of God" (vv. 18–19).

Have you ever tried to explain the Grand Canyon to someone who has never seen it? Imagine the difficulty. Try to think of an analogy for its width and height. Then explain the length and see how you do. It is pretty tough.

This, of course, is what Paul is praying for the Ephesians, that they would get even a glimpse of the Grand Canyon dimensions of God's love for them. You can only get a picture of His love, however, from reading the things that God has said about you in His Word and then believing it. *Point two: God knows you and loves you very much!*

Perhaps the most practical demonstration of these two points comes in what God did for you in Jesus Christ. Imagine going into a furniture store. Some pieces are worth a hundred dollars, and some are worth ten thousand. But the fact that they are priced differently may not mean much to you personally. You may look at the ten-thousand-dollar dining room set and wonder why in the world anyone would pay that much for it. On the other hand, you may decide it is worth that amount and sacrifice your money for it. But it has no value to you until you decide to pay for it. Biblically, when God looked at you, you had the highest price tag ever. Without hesitation, He paid that price because you are worth it!

You see, because all of us have sinned, His justice demanded a punishment. The punishment according to His Law is eternal separation from Him. But He loved you so much that He sent His Son to die for us and spill His blood so that you and I might not be separated from Him and He would have the pleasure of intimacy with us for eternity. Imagine, He loved you so much that He paid the highest price ever paid to have a personal relationship with you! Imagine the value He places on you! Imagine, too, His joy in having fellowship with you! *Point three: Your value to God can be seen in the purchase price He paid to have fellowship with you for eternity.*

So, as you see, with all the scorecards on personal worth that you face, it is crucial that you look at the right one. In God's eyes you are a 10. If you try to prove yourself to others, you will find them fickle, and you will never feel lasting value. Instead, God invites you to see yourself the way He does.

"God sees your value regardless of your performance."

The world will evaluate you on performance. God sees your value regardless of your performance. Certainly, He wants you to follow His commands. But your worth is not based on your obedience. Like salvation, it is a gift to be accepted by faith. No matter what you do as a Christian, you will always have eternal life—you will always be a son or daughter of God. That status will never change.

The same is true in terms of your personal worth. God's view is the same no matter what your performance. The epistle to the

Galatians will confirm this point. *Point four: Your worth before God is not dependent on your performance.*

Men or women whose sense of significance comes from God are secure. They realize that they can largely ignore the scorecards the world gives and can accept God's view. If there is no one to impress and nothing to prove, they work hard out of a *love for Christ* and a *love for people.* And hand in hand with accepting your value before God is accepting your weaknesses and failures in the same way He does.

It may be a shock to you to learn that God does not expect perfection from you. He is not an angry God who holds out a hammer, waiting for you to make a mistake so He can smash your fingers and reject you and punish you. Instead, God knows where you are weak and accepts you as you are:

> For as high as the heavens are above the earth,
> So great is His lovingkindness toward those
>   who fear Him.
> As far as the east is from the west,
> So far has He removed our transgressions from us.
> Just as a father has compassion on his children,
> So the LORD has compassion on those
>   who fear Him.
> *For He Himself knows our frame;* He is mindful
>   that we are but dust.
>   (Psalm 103:11–14, emphasis added)

You see, God knows that in this life no person will ever be perfect. If God waited for Christians to be perfect before He loved them or accepted them, He would still be waiting.

My children will never be perfect until they go to heaven. And neither will His. Surely, like any other parent, I am trying to help them grow. They stumble and fall just as I do, but that is only reasonable and to be expected. Even as human and limited as I am, I can't imagine ever rejecting them for making mistakes.

Sometimes I do get angry, and then I need to forgive them. But God has already forgiven you and me ahead of time. Nothing we do in the future will surprise an all-knowing God. He forgave us all of our sin—past, present, and future. That's why Romans 8 says: "Who shall bring a charge against God's elect?" and "Who shall separate us from the love of Christ?" (vv. 33, 35). The answer is no one and nothing.

"In God's view you can never be a loser."

Even as imperfect as you and I are, He will never condemn us or reject us: "There is now no condemnation for those who are in Christ Jesus" (Romans 8:1).

In God's view you can never be a loser, never so irritate Him that He rejects you. He may not always approve of what you do, but He will always love you and will not forsake you: "I will never desert you nor will I ever forsake you" (Hebrews 13:5). *Point five: God does not expect perfection nor does he withhold His approval when you fail.*

These truths are more than freeing—they are life changing. Fundamentally, they can allow you to accept yourself the way you are.

When I was an instructor pilot in the Air Force, we had an expression for students who could fly a single-seat fighter. We said they had the "right stuff." They were blessed with the talents needed to navigate and handle the ordnance of a highly maneuverable supersonic plane. The ability was a gift. It was not simply having the right attitude. Many had a good attitude but couldn't qualify for a fighter aircraft. These abilities are simply gifts that God has bestowed on some. Of course, many failed to recognize that it was God who bestowed such gifts and that only God could get the credit for the "right stuff." A rebuke for such arrogance was given to the Corinthians by Paul: "For who regards you as superior? And what do you have that you did not receive? But if you received it, why do you boast as if you had not received it?" (1 Corinthians 4:7).

The idea that emerges, then, is that you and I have been blessed with a unique set of talents given by God. On one hand, we need to give God the credit for our strengths, but we must accept our limitations and lack of ability as coming from God too. A key to self-acceptance is acknowledging God's gift of the mix of strengths and weaknesses and accepting this mixture with gratitude, not grumbling. Talents can be improved through training and practice. But your basic abilities cannot be changed. *Point six: God is the one responsible for your basic mix of strengths and weaknesses.*

So then how do you handle mistakes and failures? You see them as God sees them. First, many failures of businesses and of careers involve several factors outside a person's control. Certainly, you cannot take responsibility for the economy, interest rates, changing market conditions, and corporate takeovers.

But even when you make a mistake, it is *only* a mistake. It is not a statement about your worth as a person.

Let me tell you about one of the most painful experiences of my career, one that forced me to learn this lesson. I mentioned this in the introduction.

Four years ago, my wife and I dreamed about having a daily radio program to inspire people driving to work to honor Christ in their careers. Nothing like this was on the air.

The dream became a reality. By last year, nearly two hundred stations were carrying a daily program called "Christianity at Work." However, our ministry faced a severe economic crisis. As the economy suffered in Texas, donations to this radio ministry also suffered. Over a period of fifteen months, our donations in Texas declined 90 percent! Real estate, banking, and oil were in a recession. It was clear to our board that we could not sustain the radio program, and it was discontinued.

For months after the program stopped, we received letters and comments expressing disappointment and regret that we could not continue. I was told that the listening audience was estimated at 225,000. I read and reread letters from listeners that shared how God had used the program in a special way. I felt like a total failure. I took responsibility for disappointing each one of these people.

But as I brought all this before the Lord, a few conclusions emerged. First, I could not take full responsibility for the demise of this program. Second, I realized that while I could identify some mistakes, these mistakes did not explain why the program

---

**"When you make a mistake,
it is only a mistake. It is not a statement
about your worth as a person."**

---

was discontinued. They were regrettable, but none were in the area of integrity. I was naive and young, but my mistakes are not a statement of my personal worth. God is ultimately responsible for the outcome of my career and everyone else's. I can accept mistakes and move on. I still do feel sad, but I can accept God's will and accept myself as far less than perfect.

Others, however, may not see it this way. In fact, one sincere person suggested that the demise of the program must be because of some "sin" in my life. He did not elaborate on what sin he thought was worthy of such punishment from God. Maybe he was right. Even if he was, however, I can accept that I am a sinner and that I fail like everyone else. But the mistakes I made were only mistakes. *Point seven: Mistakes and failures are not statements of your worth.*

Somehow, though, it appears that we all tend to compare ourselves to others. Most often the comparison is both unfavorable and unfair and almost always leaves us feeling insignificant.

Perhaps God has gifted another salesman with more abilities and better opportunity. What does that say about you? Nothing.

Your worth and your performance are not linked to the performance of another. Often the person who does "better" than you at work, may not have done as well in a nonwork area. But no matter. You should be able to celebrate someone else's victories without making a comparison that is unfavorable to your personal worth. *Point eight: Comparison is usually unfavorable and unfair and leads to the illusion of insignificance.*

To summarize, significance is a status accepted as we see ourselves the way God sees us. His scorecard of our worth should be the only one we look at to check how we are doing. But shifting from seeing significance man's way to seeing it God's way does not happen automatically, nor can this view be fully grasped overnight. These truths sink in slowly, and pain assists the learning process by showing us the futility of trying to establish our own worth.

The road to significance is to accept it by faith just as you did when you became a Christian.

YOUR FAITH MAY HAVE
TO OVERRIDE YOUR FEELINGS

Perhaps at this point you can nod with agreement about what has been said, but the lingering issue is how do you get your feelings to align with your faith? First, let's look at some of the feelings we all have that challenge our sense of worth.

We all face two major fears that are the root of most stress and anxiety. The first of these is the fear of insignificance. Its three major components are the fear of failure, the fear of criticism, and the fear of embarrassment.

Sarah is about to go to her first job interview. She senses that getting a job is a cultural mark of making it as an adult. She is worried about how she will feel if she goofs the interview. She fears failure, and two minutes before she goes in for the interview, she finds her anxiety very high. She fears failure as a person more than failure to do well in the interview.

On the positive side, the fear of failure can boost performance and urge us to work hard. But the larger side of this fear is very dark and leads to unnecessary stress. Suppose you had a decision to make on buying a coffee maker. You saw it for sale for fourteen dollars. This seemed like a good price to you, but you thought you saw one advertised for thirteen dollars elsewhere. How much would you worry about buying the fourteen-dollar product? Not much. Why? Because all you had at risk was a dollar—the difference between the two prices, if you remembered it right. But suppose you were looking at a fifteen-thousand-dollar

---

"If you connect your performance to your worth, you'll be in for a stressful career ride because so many factors outside your control could cause you to fail."

---

car and wondered if it was the best price. You might be a lot more worried about making the right choice because you have so much more at risk.

Your self-worth is very important to your overall well-being. Anything that threatens it, like failure, is going to cause high anxiety. Again, if you connect your performance to your worth, you'll be in for a stressful career ride because so many factors outside your control could cause you to fail. But once your worth is established in God's view of you, then you will have less at risk and correspondingly less anxiety.

Many live with an acute consciousness of what other people think about them. Such insecurity is brought to you by the fear of criticism. If you buy the fact that your worth is only kept afloat by the composite and individual opinions of others, the thought of being criticized is very painful. It leaves you feeling insecure and worried about what they might do, or not do, to sink the public opinion boat that carries your self-worth. As mistakes are made, and they always will be, this fear is realized.

A recent luggage commercial did an excellent job of playing on a fear we all have, the fear of public embarrassment. The commercial shows a businessman entering a plane that is nearly completely filled. Overhead luggage compartments are filled too. As the man enters with what looks like a large hang-up bag, all the other passengers break out laughing. The businessman is mortified as 110 people laugh at his foolishly bringing such a large piece of luggage on the plane so late. The point of the commercial is that you should buy the sponsor's hang-up bag because it is small enough to fit under your seat and prevent such embarrassment. It plays effectively on a fear we all have.

The fear of insignificance can be very strong and can drive us in our work. It can also destroy a person's self-worth and leave him feeling insecure and very stressed. This fear will lead you away from God as you try to do something to feel good about yourself as a substitute for accepting what God says about you.

The second major fear is the fear of rejection. This too can be broken down into three component fears: the fear of peer group indifference, the fear of a low opinion of the "unspoken" crowd, and the fear of criticism or conflict.

You likely can relate to these in some way. They are really different forms of fearing what others think of you. Often we worry about our career performance, our look, our clothes, and other qualities that our peers might see.

The unspoken crowd is the group we see and never speak to. As I noted earlier, we buy what we don't need with money we don't have to impress people we don't know. Sounds a little absurd, but there is truth here. We worry about what people think about us even if we don't know them.

The fear of criticism leads many to be defensive and to resist critical remarks. A pastor was recently given an evaluation that many pastors would have envied. Yet two areas for improvement were listed. This otherwise gracious man became furious. The critique of his performance hit a very sensitive spot. Normally, we like the adage that criticism is more blessed to give than to receive.

So, with these negative emotions aroused every day, how does God's view of our worth affect how we feel? What can we do to overcome these fears?

First, we must admit our fear honestly and openly to God and to ourselves. If you are feeling nervous about a meeting at work, think about why you feel that way. Are you afraid of embarrassment, of criticism, of rejection? If so, just admit it and talk to God about it.

Second, review what God says about it. Think through the concepts presented in this chapter concerning how you score your worth.

Third, pray and ask God for His help to see yourself the way He does. Ask Him for peace in the midst of your anxiety.

Fourth, take responsible action. Don't run away from your fear. If you fear making a phone call to a prospective client, realize your fear and make the call. If you are out of work and are afraid to tell your spouse or friends, admit your fear to yourself and God; then tell them and ask for their support. If you feel

---

"Face your fears directly, but don't let them lead you to irresponsible action or keep you from doing what is right."

---

insignificant about your wardrobe, don't go in debt for what you don't need. If you worry about whether you are keeping pace with your peer group, fine. Admit your fear, but don't let it drive you to workaholism to try to allay it. Face your fears directly, but don't let them lead you to irresponsible action or keep you from doing what is right. Recall the discussion on escape hatches in chapter 1. Don't use them!

GOING DEEP

As you can see, this chapter is not for those who want a superficial quick fix. It is about the basic sense of value you place on yourself. Its focus is on accepting your worth as a gift rather than earning it through your work. It focuses, too, on how your faith can help you overcome feelings of insignificance or rejection. These truths will require more than a quick pass to grasp and implement. Too, don't be surprised if every time you read this chapter God shows you something new about yourself.

REVIEW

Main Idea: Your personal significance should be defined by God and not by your achievement or what people think about you.

Key Points:

- True significance is not measured by human judges.
- True significance comes from accepting God's view of your worth.
- Significance, like salvation, is accepted as a gift and can never be earned.

> **Point One:** God made you and is very proud of what He has made.
>
> **Point Two:** God knows you and loves you very much.
>
> **Point Three:** Your value to God can be seen in the purchase price He paid to have fellowship with you for eternity.
>
> **Point Four:** Your worth before God is not dependent on your performance.

Point Five: God does not expect perfection, nor does He withhold His approval when you fail.

Point Six: God is the one responsible for your basic mix of strengths and weaknesses.

Point Seven: Mistakes and failures are not statements of your worth.

Point Eight: Comparison is usually unfavorable and unfair and leads to the illusion of insignificance.

- Your faith may have to override your feelings.
  1. Two fundamental fears must be overcome.
     a. the fear of insignificance
     b. the fear of rejection
  2. Four steps are necessary to conquer these fears with faith.
     a. Admit your fear to God and yourself.
     b. Consider your worth and value in the light of God's Word.
     c. Pray and ask for help.
     d. Take responsible action.

STUDY OR DISCUSSION QUESTIONS

Part One
(20–30 minutes)

1. Beside each of the following statements, rate your belief in them on a scale of 1–10. The number 1 represents complete disbelief; 10 represents complete confidence and belief.

   ☐ God made you and is very proud of what He has made.

   ☐ God knows you and loves you very much.

   ☐ Your value to God can be seen in the purchase price He paid to have fellowship with you for eternity.

   ☐ Your worth before God is not dependent on your performance.

☐ God does not expect perfection, nor does He withhold His approval when you fail.

☐ God is the one responsible for your basic mix of strengths and weaknesses.

☐ Mistakes and failures are not statements of your worth.

☐ Comparison is usually unfavorable and unfair and leads to the illusion of insignificance.

2. Pick out the two areas with the lowest number rating. Why do you think you have trouble believing these truths?

Part Two
(20 minutes)

1. Describe the most secure person you know.

2. What new insights did you gain about your sense of worth and significance in this chapter?

3. Do you agree that insecure people are driven to the tops of organizations by a fear of insignificance?

4. What advice would you give to the following people?
   - a person who was laid off and feels like a failure
   - a person in midlife whose dreams of making it to the top may never come true
   - a person devastated by a low employee evaluation

5. Do you agree/disagree that ego stress and debt are connected? If so, how?

OPTIONAL

Read the following passages and list the truths you find about how God views you: Psalm 139; Ephesians 1–3; Romans 8.

— VI

HOLDING YOUR CAREER WITH A LIGHT TOUCH

"For I know the plans I have for you," declares the LORD, "plans for welfare and not for calamity to give you a future and a hope."

JEREMIAH 29:11

I trust that by now you have a new and fresh look at both your career and yourself. You have been called by God to serve Him in a tough secular world. Unlike the rest of the marketplace, you can play by different rules and be propelled by a motivation that originates with God.

One of the most compelling characteristics of true followers of Christ is that they have a peace and stability even in rough times. In part, they have learned that their self-worth is not on the line every day at work. They are secure, confident. They know that an unseen hand shapes the events of their everyday work.

The focus of this chapter is to help you have this kind of inner peace and stability. Its design is to give you a formula for happiness in the midst of changing and often difficult work situations. Fundamentally, it will offer you an approach to trust God for the results of your work and to relax. Relaxing about the results of your work each day is what I call "holding your career with a light touch."

It is a dynamically different way of seeing your work.

If you can learn to hold your career with a light touch, you will enjoy your career more, be able to turn off work when you get home, experience less stress, and enjoy greater intimacy with Christ.

I would like to offer six principles that you can use to help you hold your career with a light touch. Think of the TRIALS acrostic:

Thank God for what you have rather than complain about what you lack.

Remember God's previous faithfulness to you.

Implore God for His help today, and keep your focus on one day at a time.

Accept God's right to direct the events in your life.

Leave the future to God.

Seek Christlike character more than comfort and convenience.

These principles can be reviewed easily as you drive to work tomorrow.

They are truths that you will have to practice and practice and practice. The more you practice them, the more your character will change.

THANK GOD FOR WHAT YOU HAVE RATHER THAN COMPLAIN ABOUT WHAT YOU LACK

Have you ever taken a group of kids to the amusement park? Let's review the drill for just a moment.

First, you go down to the bank and get a second mortgage on your home. Pocketing this wad of cash, you pile those squeaky-clean little faces into the car for the trip. In our case in Washington, the park we go to is about an hour and a half south. By the

---

**"Your attitude is your choice.
You can choose to be grateful or
you can choose to grumble."**

---

time we get there, the kids have worked themselves into a fever pitch of excitement. They are loud and they are ready.

Of course, we leave early enough to get there when the park opens at eight-thirty in the morning. Otherwise, we would miss something! Then "the day" begins. You go up and down; you get wet and then go on air-conditioned boat rides with skeletons and mechanical slimy things that jump out at you. You pay twelve dollars per child for a Coke and a hot dog that is only half eaten in the flurry to get back to all the fun.

You stand in line and sweat with other people. Some, you wish had used Dial!

Then comes the "Magic Moment." You turn to those faces and say, "It's five-thirty. We have time for just one more ride." If you have kids, you know the response. They gently turn to you with a short speech that goes something like this: "Dad, we are *so* grateful for all we got to do today. We know it cost a lot of money, and we can't thank you enough. You are such a swell dad! Sure, we wish we could go on twenty more rides but one more ride would be just great!" Is that what the speech would sound like? Well, not exactly.

In fact, most parents would endure a barrage that starts with pleading and quickly degenerates into a discussion of how you have ruined their day, how every other kid in the world gets to stay at the park until nine at night (they take a poll, honest), and by the way, why can't you think of someone else for a change?

Sound familiar? If you have an adolescent in your home, the hair on the back of your neck is probably standing straight up right now.

But you know, we are not much different with our heavenly Father. Think of all that He has done for you. You are rich!

Has He given you eternal life?

Has He given you people who love you?

Did you eat today?

You can imagine that we could go on and on. With all the immeasurable blessings He has given us, why do we still complain? We are just like the kids at the park. Our focus tends to be on what we lack rather than what we have. We can even get angry at God because He has not done enough for us lately.

People who are very wealthy can grumble as loudly as people without much means. A person with a Mercedes can complain about not having a new one or not having a Rolls Royce. Rather than having immeasurable gratitude for what he has, man complains about what he doesn't have. Our appetites are insatiable.

People with nice homes complain that they can't have newer ones. People on vacation wish they had a better one.

But the one sure-fire way to learn to be content is to cultivate gratitude for what you have. Gratitude involves a regular and recurring assessment of what God has done and is doing and the practice of saying thanks to Him. Thanksgiving is one of my favorite holidays, but it was meant to be a daily practice.

Your attitude is your choice. You can choose to be grateful or you can choose to grumble.

Consider the situation of the early Hebrews. God had done a "few" things for Israel. In their generation, He had appointed a leader for the nation, Moses, who would work miracles to get them out of Egypt. God caused the Red Sea to part, caused the pursuing army to drown, and led the Israelites with a spectacular cloud. They were given a special law that revealed His will for them. Of course, He gave them food and drink and promised them a land filled with milk and honey when they had passed through the wilderness.

Was this enough for our early Jewish brothers and sisters? N-o-o-o-o! This was not enough. Israel went on to complain about the menu.

> The rabble with them began to crave other food, and again the Israelites started wailing and said, "If only we had meat to eat! We remember the fish we ate in Egypt at no cost—also the cucumbers, melon, leeks, onions, and garlic. But now we have lost our appetite; we never see anything but this manna!"
>
> Moses heard the people of every family wailing, each at the entrance to his tent. The Lord became exceeding angry, and Moses was troubled. (Numbers 11:4–6, 10)

God was angry at Israel just as I am angry when my children have a temper tantrum because after 238 rides at an amusement park they get only one more. God had provided manna daily for the people. But they complained because they didn't have the kind of food they wanted, rather than showing gratitude for what they did have.

A simple project could revolutionize your view of your life and your happiness. Make a list of all your assets—the things that are of tremendous value to you. You could write down your health, a personal relationship with Christ, perhaps a good marriage, or close friends. The value assets in your own mind can transform your perspective on life.

Assuming you are a Christian, your most important and valuable asset is a personal relationship with Christ. If you really value this relationship, Jesus Christ will dominate the landscape of your life. If your relationship with Him is distant and flabby and you are facing a financial or career squeeze, then you are headed for some rough times.

In one of my favorite books, *The Pursuit of God*, A. W. Tozer (Wheaton, Ill.: Tyndale House Publishers, 20) said:

> The man or woman who has God for his treasure has all things in one. Many ordinary things may be denied him, or if he's allowed to have them, the enjoyment of them would be so tem-

pered that they will never be necessary for his happiness. Or if he must see them go one after one, he will scarcely feel the sense of loss. For having the source of all things, he has in one all satisfaction, all pleasure, all delight. Whatever he may lose, he has actually lost nothing. For now he has it all in one, that one being Jesus Christ. And he has it purely, legitimately, and forever.

Today, you could actually begin to make a decision to focus your mind on the things God has given rather than complain about what you lack. Concentrate on all that Christ has done for you and make your relationship with Him the centerpiece of your values.

In addition, there are so many "things" to be grateful for. You may be stressed out about making a promotion. Instead you could focus on being grateful for the fact that you have a job or that you have made it as far as you have. If your business or career is doing poorly and you might have to move out of your home, you can be grateful for having it as long as you have. This principle can be applied in all situations no matter where you are. In many ways, happiness is a choice: a choice of gratitude.

It is a choice to be grateful for what you have rather than complaining about what you lack. Your happiness is directly related to the number of times per day you thank God for what He has given you.

The idea of remembering the past comes along with this principle.

REMEMBER GOD'S PREVIOUS FAITHFULNESS TO YOU

Mike is a very conscientious businessman. He does not have much debt and always pays his bills on time. In fact, he had made timely payments on a bank loan for ten years. Recently his banker called him in and demanded the balance due. Due to the savings and loan crisis, the bank became skittish about all its outstanding loans and decided to close his account. Mike was both furious and hurt. He and his family had done business at this bank for years—with no late payments. This sign of distrust was very hard to understand. In its short-sighted view, the bank forgot that Mike had been a faithful customer. Mike changed banks to find one with a longer memory. Can you feel what he felt?

Yet often when we face uncertainty or difficulty, we tend to forget God's previous faithfulness to us. We ask, "Well, what have You done for us lately?" Suddenly our memory becomes like a child's magic slate that is lifted and erases everything on it. We forget that our God was faithful to us in the past, and this causes us to doubt Him for the future.

You might be surprised to learn that "remembering" was a key issue in the Old Testament. In fact, the demise of Israel, was due in large part to their tripping over this important principle.

Hegel once said, "Man learns one thing from history, that man learns nothing from history." The nation of Israel displays this, and we can gain some important insight from their mistakes (1 Corinthians 10:1–11).

The list of miracles and blessings God brought upon this nation is long and amazing. God chose them as His people, made a covenant with them, saved them from slavery, gave them a promised land, protected them from their enemies, gave them leaders, fed and clothed them, and saved them from calamity. He told them to remember these miracles and God's faithfulness to them (Exodus 13:3; Deuteronomy 5:15; 15:15; 16:12; 18:22; 32:7). In fact, God established both the Passover and the Sabbath as regular occasions to remember what God had done. It seems as though God knew that in the heart of man was a fundamental mistrust that had to be overcome by repeated reflection on God's previous faithfulness.

Nevertheless, Israel forgot what God had done and complained that He was not doing enough and doubted the continuance of His blessing. This led them to complain, to be angry at God, and ultimately to turn away from Him. That Moses' generation did not get to the Promised Land and that Israel would ultimately be taken into exile were largely due to her "forgetting" what God had done for her in the past.

Nehemiah, a prophet in the time of Israel's exile, looked back over her history and confessed to God: "And they refused to listen, and did not remember Thy wondrous deeds which Thou hast performed among them" (Nehemiah 9:17).

In another look backwards, the psalmist in Psalm 78 argues the same link between forgetting what God had done and the demise of Israel's faith and happiness.

> How often they rebelled against Him
>   in the wilderness,
> And grieved Him in the desert!
> And again and again they tempted God,
> And pained the Holy One of Israel.
> They did not remember His power,
> The day when He redeemed them
>   from the adversary,
> When He performed His signs in Egypt,
> And His marvels in the field of Zoan.
>   (Psalm 78:40–43)

The lesson we can glean from Israel, then, is that it is crucial to remember regularly how God has led you, blessed you, and fulfilled His promises to you. When trials come—and they certainly will—our confidence in Him during that time may need to be restored. Considering your personal history with God and His track record can be key. The Bible is clear: The God who was faithful to you in the past is the same God who will see you through the future. "Jesus Christ is the same, yesterday and today, yes, and forever" (Hebrews 13:8).

The third principle for having joy in the midst of difficulties relates to your daily focus, dividing life into bite-sized chunks.

IMPLORE GOD FOR HIS HELP TODAY, AND KEEP YOUR FOCUS ON ONE DAY AT A TIME

In the Lord's Prayer we are taught to pray, "Give us this day our daily bread" (Matthew 6:11).

This simple idea is foundational to surviving and enjoying each workday. God wants us to pray about the daily work issues that bring us our daily bread.

Imagine your busy work routine. Imagine the meeting at nine in the morning, the conference with the boss at ten, the lunch with a customer, the phone calls that afternoon, the project that must be done by tomorrow. Now imagine doing all this without God's help. Or rather, what difference would it make in your day if you *did* get His help?

Suppose you prayed through the events of your day as you are driving to work or in your morning prayer time.

Prayer is no guarantee that everything will go your way that day, although I have to say that more often than not I can really tell a big difference when I do pray. Prayer changes me as much

---

"God cares about your daily work—the calls, the meetings, the problems."

---

as it changes God's mind on how He will help me.

Even if I assume at a subtle level that I really don't need God's help, God has an amazing ability to remind me when the day goes poorly that I did not preview the day in prayer.

God cares about your daily work—the calls, the meetings, the problems. As our heavenly Father, He delights in our bringing issues to Him and asking for wisdom and help.

Bottom line, we show how much we think we need His help by how much we pray. In reality, our habit of prayer is one of the best litmus paper tests of what we really believe about God and ourselves.

Our next principle will separate true disciples of Christ from those who only have a casual interest in Him. It also will present another key to having real joy.

ACCEPT GOD'S RIGHT TO DIRECT
THE EVENTS IN YOUR LIFE

We have already seen that while we are primarily interested in our comfort and convenience, God is interested in our character. To refine our character and to display to a watching world His glory in the lives of those who suffer difficulty as His Son did, He permits difficulty.

Yet many respond with anger and complaint. Too often I do. But He has helped me see four simple ideas that have profound significance each workday.

1. He is Lord and has the right to do what He wishes.

2. He has a *good* purpose for everything He allows into my life.

3. I must accept His right to rule over the events of my daily work and life.

4. Everything I have belongs to Him.

Let's unpack these a little. First, Jesus Christ is Lord and has the right to rule. He:

- is the creator of Heaven and earth and all things were created for Him and His glory (Colossians 1:16);
- is worthy of all riches and might and power and dominion (Revelation 5:9–14);
- sets up nations and moves the boundaries of nations (Daniel 5; 6);
- has the keys to heaven and hell (Revelation 1:18);
- is the One who "opens and no one can shut and shuts and no one can open" (Revelation 3:7).

Of course, His position has been challenged by men in times past. Consider Job, Habakkuk, and Nebuchadnezzar, three men who challenged God's leadership in their lives—each of them came to some new conclusions.

Job suffered immeasurably. He lost his wealth, his children, his health, and more. While he kept his integrity, he asked God some of the same questions I ask when things are tough: What are you doing? Why are you doing this to me? What did I do to

---

"Accepting [God's] right to rule over the events of your day can make each day an adventure."

---

deserve this? God answered the questions with the simple idea that man has no right nor ability to critique an infinite God:

> Who is this who darkens counsel by words without knowledge? Now gird up your loins like a man and I will ask you, and you will instruct Me! Where were you when I laid the foundation of the earth! Tell me if you have understanding. . . . Have you ever commanded the morning, and caused the dawn to know its place? . . . Have you understood the expanse of the earth? Tell me if you know this. . . . Can you lift up your voice to the clouds so that an abundance of water may cover you? (Job 38:2–4, 12, 18, 34)

God's point is that as Creator and Sustainer of the universe, He is the only One with the wisdom and knowledge to run it; so He has the right to bring events into our lives. *What Job learned was that giving God the right to rule in his life involved giving Him permission to let even Job's worst nightmare come true, if that is His will.* This involves submission and the belief that if God can run the universe, He can run the events of my life.

A funny-named prophet later asked God the same questions and came to the same conclusion. Habakkuk was a prophet of Israel who had the dubious honor of telling Judah that they were about to be deported to Babylon because of their disobedience. He had real problems with God's plan at first and had some pointed questions for Him about it. God also answered this man.

After the dialogue Habakkuk recognized that God is great enough and wise enough to rule the universe.

He also discovered that there is great freedom in letting God take control, even if it means disaster. *He learned that submitting to God's leadership in his life brought joy and fulfillment that meant more to him than having prosperity.* Habakkuk said:

> Though the fig tree should not blossom and there
> be no fruit on the vines, though the yield of the
> olive should fail, and the fields produce no food,
> Though the flock should be cut off from the fold,
> and there be no cattle in the stalls yet I will exalt in
> the LORD and rejoice in the God of my salvation.
> The LORD God is my strength. (Habakkuk 3:17–18)

Finally, a pagan king learned something about God after God sent him on a camping trip alone to learn it. *Nebuchadnezzar, king of one of the greatest empires in history, learned that questioning God was a silly act of rebellion and arrogance.* At the end of his camping trip he said:

> But at the end of this period I, Nebuchadnezzar, raised my eyes toward heaven, and my reason returned to me and I blessed the Most High and praised and honored Him who lives forever; for His dominion is an everlasting dominion and His kingdom endures from generation to generation. And all the inhabitants of the earth are accounted as nothing. But He does according to His will in the host of heaven and among the inhabitants of the earth; And no one can ward off His hand or say to Him "what hast Thou done?" (Daniel 4:34, 35)

Accepting His right to rule over the events of your day can make each day an adventure. Knowing that these events come from God with a good purpose can make each day the challenge God intended. But real joy cannot begin until you accept God's leadership in your life.

The fifth principle involves your vision of the future.

LEAVE THE FUTURE TO GOD

Christianity is primarily today-oriented. This means we take life in one-day chunks and focus on one day at a time. Jesus said: "Therefore do not worry about tomorrow, for tomorrow will worry about itself. Each day has enough trouble of its own" (Matthew 6:34).

While there is nothing wrong per se about setting goals for the future, God wants us to concentrate on faithfulness to Him today. In other words, your faithfulness to Him today is more important than your faithfulness to Him tomorrow. The work before you today is more important than tomorrow. This view can take a lot of stress off your shoulders.

Fred is in a health care company that has just been bought out by some investors. The new owners are interested in thinning out the number of employees, and he is anxious about being fired. He tends to focus on the future, and the horizon looks dark. What might happen to his family? How will the mortgage be paid? What about college? What will his friends think? These looming questions tend to dominate his thinking. He gives a 40 percent effort to his present responsibilities at home and at work because he is so "wrapped around the axle."

God would say to Fred: "Fred, you need to take care of *today*. Tomorrow is my responsibility. You have enough to worry about today. Leave the future to Me. I created you with the capacity to take one day at a time. Ultimately, your job doesn't meet your needs; I do. And I will never fail you or forsake you."

Have you ever watched a triathlon on TV? This athletic event involves a swim, a bike ride, and a run of varying lengths. The swim leaves you out of breath and your upper body fatigued. The bike leaves your legs tight, tired, and sore. Then comes the run, which is between six and twenty-six miles, depending on the race. Usually the race is won or lost in the run. The key to this segment is mostly mental. If you begin to focus on how long the run is, you will quit. It is too overwhelming. Winners have learned to focus their minds on one mile at a time and to run that mile as though it were the only mile in the race, keeping an overall pace in view. Many excellent athletes get overwhelmed mentally in the run segment and stop to walk, ruining their score. They were beaten because their mental focus was too far down the road.

The Christian life is similar. If you focus too much on what will happen to you next week, you will fail today. God designed life for us in bite-sized daily chunks. Life should be lived today as if there were no tomorrow. If not, you can become overwhelmed and underperform.

Imagine two fighter-type aircraft flying three feet apart in tight formation through a wide range of maneuvers! Perhaps you have seen the Thunderbirds do this at five hundred miles an hour.

Now picture the return to base for landing. These aircraft can fly in tight formation all the way to touchdown. When the weather is poor, landing becomes a little "hairy." Let me explain.

These two aircraft in the clouds have about twenty feet of visibility. They fly very close, and the lead pilot just looks at his instruments. The number two pilot just looks at lead. When they approach the field, the two pilots will, on signal from lead, lower their landing gear, and together the aircraft change pitch like a porpoise in the water. Because the number two pilot is looking out the side of the aircraft instead of straight ahead, his sensory perception gives him funny signals as he decelerates and the nose pitches up and down. Sometimes he feels as if he is in ninety degrees of bank when he is wings level with the horizon. Now if he shifts his focus from lead to the cockpit, he could easily either slide into lead or away from lead in the clouds close to the ground. Either could be disastrous. What we as instructors had to burn into the memory of students learning to fly in bad weather is to trust lead no matter how scary it feels. "Your job," we would say, "is to follow lead and stay in position; his job is to make a safe approach." But this is tough when you feel as if the plane is in a steep bank about to crash. It involves focus and trust.

Trusting God with the future is like formation flying. Our job is to focus on today and take life one day at a time. God is responsible for the future and wants us to relax about it and trust Him.

But in some ways this is a very humbling thing to do. It involves giving up control.

Personally, I tend to want a lot of control over my future. I want to know where I will live, to set my standard of living, to go where I want, and to buy what I want. I would like to plan out my future and see that plan happen the way I imagined. However, God finds this desire to control arrogant and foolish:

> Come now you who say "Today or tomorrow, we shall go to such and such a city, and spend a year there and engage in business and make a profit." Yet you do not know what your life will be like tomorrow. You are just a vapor that appears for a while and then vanishes away. Instead, you ought to say, "If the Lord wills, we shall live and also do this or that." But as it is, you boast in your arrogance; all such boasting is evil. (James 4:13–16)

So the future must be held with a light touch, giving God full permission to bless or redirect your plans. Make career plans, but continue to say, "If the Lord wills."

The fact that we work for Jesus Christ each day is not a burden but a load lifter. Would you *really* want the responsibility of planning out the future for yourself? Do you imagine that you have the wisdom to figure the best career track for your happiness? Or the best path for your personal growth and joy? Can you remember making plans for the future only to find that God in His wisdom had a better idea for you?

So life is a little out of my control. This is the "good news" when I am thinking straight and "bad news" when I am not.

Now we come to the final principle in the TRIALS acrostic.

SEEK CHRISTLIKE CHARACTER MORE THAN COMFORT AND CONVENIENCE

Perhaps this concept summarizes much of the book so far. Consider the two lists below, and ask yourself which list means the most to you.

1. having plenty of money

2. having perfect health

3. having a smooth life relatively free from conflict or pain

4. having little stress or anxiety about the future

5. having status in your community

or

1. becoming a servant to others after the fashion of Jesus Christ

2. becoming more loving of others

3. bringing glory to God

4. having greater intimacy with Christ

5. becoming more disciplined in your speech, conduct, and thoughts, conforming to God's design for your life

It doesn't take a rocket scientist to figure out which list *should* mean more to us. But our real values are shown more by how we live than how we answer a multiple choice test. We can want them both, but which list means the most to us is evident in our lifestyle. When Jesus told us we cannot have "two masters," He was referring to the fact that one of these lists will dominate the other. Either Jesus Christ dominates the landscape of our life, or a self-centered life pursuing comfort and convenience will. Among the things at stake in this choice is our happiness. The more Christ-centered you are, the more joy you experience, even in pain. The more self-centered you are, the less fulfilled you will be, even when you are having fun.

Below is a chart that shows the difference in these two life purposes.

	When comfort and convenience matter most . . .	When Christlike character matters most . . .
You'll pray:	"Lord, make this problem go away."	"Lord, not my will but Yours be done; only help me learn to respond correctly."

	When comfort and convenience matter most . . .	When Christlike character matters most . . .
You'll think:	Why is God doing this to me? When will it be over? I'm angry at God for allowing this.	I must trust in God's good purpose and plan for me, and learn to depend on Him more.
You'll value:	Being in control of your circumstances; trusting in yourself; achievement, prestige, and peer respect.	Being dependent on God daily; a deep relationship with God that affects all other relationships; the character He is building into you.
You'll experience:	Frustration and anger because your goals are blocked.	A daily walk with Christ that involves Him in the details of your life.
Your character will be:	Superficial, self-centered, bitter, and arrogant.	That of a Christlike servant who both knows and trusts God in his or her daily experience.

As you can see, a key to your happiness is recognizing and accepting God's plan for your life to make you like His Son.

I hope the TRIALS acrostic can stay with you for years. These biblical truths make a package you can apply often. They suggest a dynamically different way of viewing life and the circumstances you endure.

You will also find that as you apply them in various situations you'll learn them in a fresh and deeper way. They can be your friends to help you through common stress or the darkest moments of your life.

REVIEW

Main Idea: God wants you to trust Him with the results of your labor each day.

Key Points:

- Thank God for what you have rather than complain about what you lack.
- Remember God's previous faithfulness to you.
- Implore God for help.
- Accept His leadership in your life.
- Leave the future to God.
- Seek Christlike character above comfort or convenience.

STUDY OR DISCUSSION QUESTIONS

Part One
(60 minutes)

1. List all the major gifts God has given you.

2. List the things you wish you had or tend to complain about.

3. Why do you think people focus on the second list rather than on the first?

4. What major events in your life have clearly shown you God's faithfulness to lead you, protect you, or provide for you?

5. What major issues must you face today?

6. What do you think is the hardest part of accepting God's leadership in your life?

7. Why do you think we all tend to want to control the future?

8. What is your greatest fear as you look to the future?

9. List what you believe to be the five most compelling character qualities of Jesus Christ.

10. What price do you think a person must pay to become like Christ?

11. What are the rewards for a person who is becoming like the Lord?

12. Describe the most Christlike person you know.

OPTIONAL

Review the TRIALS acrostic on your way to work each day this week. Review once on your way in, then again on the return trip. Record any difference in your attitude at work.

Thank God for what you have rather than complain about what you lack.

Remember God's previous faithfulness to you.

Implore God for His help today, and keep your focus on one day at a time.

Accept God's right to direct the events in your life.

Leave the future to God.

Seek Christlike character more than comfort and convenience.

PART 3

WITH A CHANGED ATTITUDE, YOU CAN TAKE THE RIGHT ACTION

— VII

YOUR SECOND FAMILY

If I speak with the tongues of men and of angels, but do not have love, I have become a noisy gong or a clanging cymbal. And if I give all my possessions to feed the poor, and if I deliver my body to be burned, but do not have love, it profits me nothing.

1 Corinthians 13:1, 3

It is sometimes a little shocking to consider how much time we spend with co-workers. If you enter the job market at twenty and retire at seventy, working an average of forty-five hours a week, then of these fifty years of adult life, you will spend twenty-two and a half of them with various co-workers. That is more time than you will spend with family or friends. For example, if you actually spent three hours a day interacting with your family, seven days a week, over the same fifty-year period, you would spend only ten years of time with them. Not quite half the time spent with co-workers! For this reason, I call your co-workers your "second family."

As in all families, difficult people and conflicts in the work world present a significant threat to your well-being. True, most families argue. But the marketplace has dark figures in shady places with big teeth! It is filled with people who play by a different set of rules than you do as a follower of Christ. Most are addicted to ego biscuits. What else is there to live for if you don't have Christ?

It's a jungle of people with their own agendas, their own interests, and you either help or hurt the pursuit of their ego biscuits. Even if they are thinly veiled, anger, envy, greed, revenge, and pride dominate the landscape of the workplace.

So how does a Christian handle a world like this? Being like them? Playing by the same rules? Business is business and religion is religion? *Nope!*

GOD WANTS YOU TO LOVE THEM!

Perhaps you thought that your job was entirely your choice and the people you work with are just there by coincidence. But the fellow workers who comprise your second family have been placed there by a sovereign God who makes no mistakes and who moves very deliberately. You are His representative to these people. You are an ambassador as though representing the king in a foreign country.

Since you represent Jesus Christ each day, let's consider how He would treat these people. First of all, He loves them deeply. While we as Christians love to celebrate His love for us on the cross, we need to remember that He died for all people (John 3:16). In fact He loved all of us, even in a state of rebellion (Romans 5:8).

Unlike human love, God's love does not demand a response. Even when people hate God, He still loves them. Jesus said, "The Most High is kind to ungrateful and evil men" (Luke 6:35b).

You see, when I am kind to others, I *expect* the same treatment. This is fair, but it is not love, and it is not God's way of doing business. He wants me to love other people regardless of their response, even if they turn out to be my enemies.

Returning to what Jesus said in Luke 6, let's look at the rest of the story: "But love your enemies and do good and lend expecting nothing in return and your reward will be great and you will be sons of the Most High; for He Himself is kind to ungrateful and evil men. Be merciful, just as your Father is merciful" (Luke 6:35–36).

You see, God wants us to love people, even our enemies, because He loves them. This is a major key to success in your relationship with the folks you work with. *We are to view people as God*

"The fellow workers who comprise your second family have been placed there by a sovereign God who makes no mistakes and who moves very deliberately."

---

sees them and to treat them as Jesus Christ would. This simple idea is the foundation for this chapter. But it is simple only in its wording. Carrying it out requires supernatural power and wisdom. Fortunately, we have a God who is patient while we stumble along trying to live up to the ideal.

"I CARE" PHILOSOPHY

So how do you show love to your co-workers? Think of your boss, a co-worker, and a customer for just a minute. Showing love for them may not involve meeting socially or lingering long over coffee discussing their personal problems on work time. But you can have a basic attitude toward them that says:

1. I am glad you are alive.

2. I wish the best for you.

3. I am willing to do what I can to help you.

Perhaps it is summed up in "I care." It may involve encouraging a co-worker who has done a good job or going out of your way to serve a customer.

Think of your relationships as constructing a building. Every time you care for people, you have placed one more brick in the building.

This basic attitude is a thing of beauty. Most people are self-centered and only love themselves. The Christian, however, reflects Christ's love for people and is kind, thoughtful, and generous. This attitude takes the strength, love, and discipline described in Philippians 2:14–15: "that you may prove yourselves to be blameless and innocent children of God above reproach in the midst of a crooked and perverse generation among whom you appear as lights in the world holding fast the word of life."

The verse portrays the Christian reflecting Christ and His character in a moral jungle. Reflecting Christlike love in a secular world is one of the highest and noblest things any man or woman could aspire to. But your reward may only come from God. Man may not compliment you or return thanks for your caring spirit. In fact to expect compliments or to look for them will not only set you up for great disappointment, it will betray the wrong motive for your actions in the first place. Being nice to others so that they will be nice to us is closer to manipulation than genuine care.

Please, do not misunderstand what I am saying. Work must be done. Your time in interacting may be limited. But you can show an "I care" attitude *if you have it in your heart.*

Here are some practical ideas.

1. Express enthusiasm to see people.

2. Smile.

3. Take time to compliment others.

4. Pray for co-workers on your way to work.

5. Take a co-worker to lunch once a week.

6. Try to offer ten positives for every negative you must give.

7. When they are sick, experience a death in the family, or have a problem, tell your co-workers that you are sorry and explore what you could do to help.

Certainly these ideas could be done for the wrong motives. Managers regularly go to seminars about how being "people oriented" can help get more work out of people. The seminars are right. But if managers or anyone else does this out of anything but a genuine love, people will see right through it.

But many people have asked me, "Well this is nice, but suppose you have no feeling for the people you work with. They

---

"Warm actions can change a cold heart. Our emotions do not respond on command, but our arms and legs do."

---

seem so self-absorbed and difficult. How do I change my feelings toward them? I want to genuinely love them, but I don't."

Several years ago a woman came to a Christian lawyer in Texas who specialized in family concerns. She was so bitter at her husband for being a schmuck. He was unfaithful and a creep. She asked the lawyer for his advice on how to take her husband to the cleaners and exact the greatest amount of pain out of him possible.

The lawyer told her that to reach her objective, she should remember all the really nice things she did for him when they were first married and in love. She was told to do these for two months and then surprise him one day with divorce papers. This would rekindle his love for her in time for her to cut the legs out from under his feet with complete rejection.

On a mission, the wife set out on the program. There were candlelight dinners, cards in the underwear drawer, breakfast in bed, a weekend away at a bed and breakfast place. She got a new wardrobe and a makeover.

Three months later the lawyer had not heard from the wife. Six months later he ran into her in a store. With a red face she told him that after she did the things he suggested, her heart melted. Her actions had rekindled a love in both her husband and herself.

The principle here is that warm actions can change a cold heart. Our emotions do not respond on command, but our arms and legs do. When you choose to do the right things toward your co-workers, you will find that your heart will follow. It may take a while, but God will honor your obedience to Him and the steps you have taken. You can also trust God for the strength and discipline required. The formula is to *take steps* and to *trust God* for help. If you do, you can develop more of Christ's love for the people with whom you work.

Now all that has been said so far has been on the positive side of your response. It is the pro-active part of your love for others. When in doubt, you can summarize and clarify by asking the Lord the simple question, "Lord Jesus, what attitude would you have me maintain toward the people I work with?"

If you will ask Him this question throughout your workday, you will be amazed at His leading!

But sometimes, in fact maybe often, how you show love is a little tricky. Just as a parent of a teenager considers how to love his child, it is not so simple as just letting the child have his way all the time. At times, love requires toughness as well as tenderness. It demands that we work through conflict, because, like death and taxes, conflict is inevitable.

To tackle the subject of difficult relationships, we will take a two-step process. First, I will lay a foundation of general principles in the rest of this chapter. Then in chapter 8, we will deal with some very specific conflicts that occur with your boss and with your fellow workers and customers.

Now let's look at some general principles of how you should deal with your anger and bitterness and effectively resolve conflicts.

SEVEN PRINCIPLES OF CONFLICT RESOLUTION

When your relationships at work are in good condition, a kind of equilibrium must be maintained and serviced. When conflict arises, you should do all that you can to restore that balance. Some people will not let you resolve conflict, but that is up to them. Your goal is to do all that you can to live at peace with all men. It takes two to have a relationship, but regardless of how others respond, you must do all you can on your side of the fence to keep that equilibrium.

Principle One: Don't Go to Sleep Angry

Different jobs involve different stress levels and have different levels of anger. But the source of most conflicts is either that someone's pride has been wounded or he has been inconvenienced or has experienced injustice. James addresses the source of conflicts this way: "What is the source of quarrels and conflicts among you? Is not the source your pleasures that wage war in your members? You lust and do not have so you commit murder. And you are envious and cannot obtain: so you fight and quarrel" (James 4:1, 2).

When our ego goals have been blocked, we get angry. If we get an unfavorable employee evaluation, we might get angry at our boss because we think she has injured our significance as a person.

If we stand in a long line at the store, we can become angry because it inconveniences us. If we don't get credit for our work, we are hot.

So what do you do about it? Here are some suggestions for diffusing your anger.

1. Ask the question, "Why am I so angry? Is it because of my pride, my selfishness, or my sense of justice?"

2. Pray about how you are feeling. Ask Christ what response He would have you make.

3. Control your tongue and do not take revenge.

4. Forgive the person with whom you are angry.

5. Take appropriate action.

Let's say you are the manager of a large restaurant. The owner calls you up and vigorously chews you out because late yesterday a friend got a cold meal. You say you don't know anything about it and that you'll look into it. You feel angry at the owner for the way you were chewed out and at the waiter for making you look bad.

First, why are you so mad? Well, you begin to reason it out and find that a lot of it is just pride. Your boss gave you what you felt was an idiot message. Or in other words you felt you got an "insignificant" or "incompetent" message. Understandably, you would be upset. But as we have already seen, she is not the one who will evaluate you nor do you need to prove anything to her. The owner took away an ego biscuit, that's all. Something you don't need anyway. Thus the source of your anger is that you are being kept from proving your worth. This is just pride.

As you pray about it, you confess your anger and its source, your pride, to Christ and ask for wisdom and help. You ask in a brief silent prayer, "Lord Jesus, what attitude would you have me maintain right now?" As you do this, you will have a pretty clear impression of His answer.

Then you go to your waiter and find out what happened. You don't make accusations; you just try to find out what happened. Trying to sort out the truth is tough, but you tell the waiter that it must not happen again, and if necessary you mention that there are standards for all employees and that to keep the job he must meet the standards. He may not understand or appreciate it, but your goal is to respond correctly regardless of how anyone else responds. In any case, you handle the situation with fairness and measured responses—even when the waiter is defensive.

But you still owe an explanation to the boss even though you're angry at her. Ask yourself why the boss was angry. In this case knowing that she was embarrassed can be of some help. Your real challenge, though, is to explain what the waiter did—or did not do—without becoming angry or defensive yourself. You avoid responding in anger. You see, anger has a way of blowing a small issue up into a major problem. When you are mad at someone, you tend to put on negative "glasses," almost expecting that person to do something that will make you angrier. Negative anticipation can cause you to overstate your case and escalate a conflict from a small skirmish to World War III! That's why Proverbs 15:1 says, "A gentle answer turns away wrath but a harsh word stirs up anger."

So in a controlled voice you apologize to the boss for the action or inaction of the waiter and explain what you intend to do to keep it from happening again. If you can accept responsibility for any of what happened, do that too. Be respectful.

Let's say, though, that after all this has happened, you still have some hard feelings toward the owner. You may need to take some time to pray about her and forgive her from the heart.

No matter what has happened to you, your first step is to forgive. In Matthew 18:21–35, you will find Peter asking Jesus how many times he should forgive someone who wrongs him. The answer is well known but infrequently practiced: seventy times seven. Jesus then goes on to say that from heaven's perspective, it is a little odd that the King of the universe has forgiven us for a lifetime of rebellion, yet we have difficulty forgiving relatively minor offenses.

Perhaps this, then, is the starting point for forgiveness: to consider all that Christ has forgiven you and then to let another's offense pale in comparison.

A second way to get perspective is to remind yourself of how Christ loves and accepts this person. The simple fact that Christ died for her lends an amazing perspective to the value of an individual.

Third, you need to know that forgiving a person is not easy. At times it can be one of the most difficult struggles you face. At one moment you might feel victory over anger, and then in another, anger rears its ugly head again and you have to repeat the whole process.

Scripture memory can be extraordinarily helpful to you in overcoming anger (1 John 4:11; James 3:17, 18; 4:1).

Sometimes forgiving a person and pursuing justice may be two different things. Let's say that you are a salesman for an office supply company. You were not given some of the commission money you earned. This caused some real hardship for you and your family. Understandably, you are upset.

Your first step when wronged is to forgive. But there is no reason you cannot pursue legal remedies or even contact the owner of the company, if necessary, to get the money you deserve.

Anger is a fire that can quickly blaze out of control. The Bible makes it clear that your anger should be dealt with before you put your head on the pillow. Tomorrow may bring a whole new set of challenges, but each day's anger should be dealt with "before the sun goes down" (Ephesians 4:26). If you are angry, don't try to pretend you are not. But put out the fire quickly.

As you mature in Christ, you will gain a longer and longer fuse. You'll sort the big fish from the little fish.

But if you don't douse the fire, you may develop a four-alarm case of bitterness.

Principle Two: Guard Yourself Against the Toxic Waste of Bitterness

People who have no intention of dousing the flames of anger turn bitter. The bitter person so revels in his anger that his ill thoughts of another actually give him a kind of rank pleasure. Subtly he thinks that by being angry he is inflicting pain on the person who wronged him. But his anger actually boomerangs and injures himself and the people around him. In Hebrews God says, "Pursue peace with all men, and the sanctification without which no one will see the Lord. See to it that no one comes short of the grace of God; that no root of bitterness springing up causes trouble, and by it many be defiled" (12:14–15).

Bitterness is a self-generated, highly toxic acid that can ruin your life. But it can also ruin the lives of people around you, thus "defiling" many.

Do you remember the teacher in chapter 1 who got a low performance rating that shattered her dream of being a principal? Her bitterness not only was affecting her sleep and eating habits but was also the dominant theme of every discussion with friends and family. They too tended to pick up a bitterness toward the principal. They also became tired of hearing about it and of her absorption with the problem.

When you are bitter, the starting point is to forgive. You might want to have a few close friends pray for you. As I suggested earlier, memorize Scripture and review it throughout the day. Your anger tends to be a kind of Jack-in-the-box that, even if

---

"As you mature in Christ, you will gain a longer and longer fuse. . . . But if you don't douse the fire, you may develop a four-alarm case of bitterness."

---

it is put down, tends to pop up throughout the day. Victory over it may require a spiritual wrestling match for days on end. But in Christ you can have victory. So keep up the fight!

I just can't emphasize this enough. Bitterness is a choice God wants you to avoid because He loves you. It's not correct to say, "This person made me bitter," like Flip Wilson's "The devil made me do it!" No one can "make" you angry and bitter. It is your choice. It may be a long hard fight, but you have in Christ all the resources you need to win. And *you must win!*

Principle Three: If You Have Offended Someone, Quickly Seek Reconciliation

Yes, it's true. It is possible that wonderful, godly people like you and me can offend others. It might be a misunderstanding or something we have done that is truly wrong. In any case, the biblical answer is to *quickly* go to that person and do what you can to restore the relational equilibrium.

Here's what Jesus said.

If therefore you are presenting your offering at the altar, and there remember your brother has something against you, leave your offering there before the altar and go your way; first be reconciled to your brother and then come and present your offering. Make friends with your opponent at law while you are with him on the way, in order that your opponent may not deliver you to the judge, and the judge to the officer, and you be thrown into prison. (Matthew 5:23–25)

Jesus makes two points in this sermon. First, from heaven's perspective, the priority on reconciliation is so high that you should interrupt your prayer time or whatever you are doing for Christ to go and reconcile. His second point is that it is best for you to reconcile as early as possible. The sooner the better because conflict and anger tend to escalate and reinforce themselves over time.

Often an offense can be corrected by a simple apology, if appropriate. Sometimes miscommunication must be ironed out. The point is, if you have inadvertently—or maybe even deliberately— caused an offense, you take the initiative to resolve it.

Principle Four: When Insulted or Mistreated, Respond Under Control Without Escalating the Conflict

If an angry customer comes in upset and asks an insulting question, respond under control with a gentle, respectful answer. Doing this usually diffuses the conflict at least a little. Proverbs has a wealth of wisdom on conflict resolution.

> A gentle answer turns away wrath, but a harsh
> word stirs up anger.
> > (Proverbs 15:1)

> A hot-tempered man stirs up strife, but the slow to
> anger pacifies contention.
> > (Proverbs 15:18)

You can't control other people. You can, with Christ's help, control your response. A gentle response generally will keep the conflict from escalating.

"Humility is a quality of character that comes from knowing that you do not look to man for your worth and you do not have to protect your ego. This is real strength!"

You show tremendous strength of character when you don't get upset at little things. A self-centered or insecure person cannot do this. He must protect his ego. Proverbs says, "He who is slow to anger is better than the mighty, and he who rules his spirit, than he who captures a city" (Proverbs 16:32).

The strength of a conquering king is less than that of a man who can control his anger. This inner strength is humility. It does not mean you have to become a doormat. Instead, humility is a quality of character that comes from knowing that you do not look to man for your worth and you do not have to protect your ego. This is *real* strength!

Principle Five: Revenge Is Not Sweet; Don't Taste It!

All that has been said so far about loving co-workers and dealing with anger and bitterness still leaves one question on the table: What about justice? As you will see in a minute, you can pursue justice if you go about it in the right way and if you pick the right issues.

A recent *Wall Street Journal* article reported: "The decade of downsizing has triggered another legacy: revenge. A growing number of employees are retaliating (or fantasizing about it) for past or perceived wrongs. They are taking it out on colleagues, bosses or their companies in general" ("Sweet Revenge is Souring the Office," *Wall Street Journal,* 19 Sept. 1990).

But revenge is not new. It is a part of the human nature to retaliate swiftly against whoever hurt us with as much pain as we can get by with. God calls this out of bounds for man. God says that all revenge should be in His domain, not ours. Our mandate is never to return evil for evil: "Never pay back evil for evil to anyone. Never take your own revenge, beloved, but leave room for the wrath of God, for it is written, 'Vengeance is Mine, I will repay,' says the Lord" (Romans 12:17, 19).

We really get chafed when someone does something wrong and it *appears* they suffer no consequences. Then we want to spring into action and play God.

Revenge can be as violent as shooting a boss who just laid off a worker, but more than likely it takes more subtle forms: bad-mouthing the boss to others, showing up late for meetings, deliberately trying to exclude a person from a responsible position. Usually, such actions can be rationalized under some kind of pretense. But a thoughtful and prayerful Christian can go to God and ask, "Lord, am I about to take revenge or responsible action?" The answer may become clear in your conscience.

Admittedly, revenge is quite understandable. But while it is an understandable instinct, it is wrong. Instead, God wants us to trust that even if it appears that justice was not done, ultimately it will be—in His time and in His way.

Principle Six: Go the Extra Mile with People; Don't Make a Federal Case Out of a Misdemeanor

Certainly there is room to "go through channels" to resolve a grievance or even to personally confront a person. In some situations you may even need to go to court to settle an issue. But pick your issues carefully and only make a big deal out of big deals. Biblically, God wants us to have a long fuse and to be patient with others' faults. Jesus said:

You have heard that it was said, "an eye for an eye and a tooth for a tooth." But I say to you do not resist him who is evil, but whoever hits you on the right cheek, turn to him the other also. And if anyone wants to sue you, and take your shirt, let him have your coat also. And whoever shall force you to go one mile, go with him two. (Matthew 5:38–41)

The point is to do all you can to achieve relational equilibrium even when it seems a little unfair.

But if the injustice involves your career or a major issue, then you can feel the freedom to pursue justice through appropriate means—even going to court. You were told to go the extra mile, not twenty!

Principle Seven: Do All You Can, But Don't Take Responsibility for Another's Response

Try as you might to avoid conflict and to restore broken relationships, it is possible and likely that your efforts will not succeed. For example, if you are a boss and you had to fire an employee, there may be nothing you can say or do to keep that person from hating you. But that is up to the other person. Your responsibility is to mow the grass on your side of the fence, not on his. If a conflict is not resolved, then go to bed knowing that you did all you could to bring about restoration. That is all that the Lord asks of us.

BE A FRENCH HORN, NOT A CLANGING CYMBAL

Your relationships at work are a good litmus paper test of how close you are to Christ and how well you know Him. The Christian life is primarily reflected in relationships with God and with our fellow men. *The person who is weak in relationships is a weak Christian.*

If you feel your relationships need strengthening, begin by reviewing the Scripture discussed in this chapter, and then ask Christ many times throughout your workday tomorrow, what attitude He would have you maintain and what He would have you do.

REVIEW

Main Idea: You are to reflect Christ's love toward your co-workers even in your efforts to resolve tension and conflict.

Key Points:

- Your co-workers are your second family, and God wants you to love them.
- You should take an "I care" philosophy to work with you.
    1. I am glad you are alive.
    2. I want the best for you.
    3. I am willing to do all I can to help you.
- Follow seven principles of conflict resolution.
    1. **Principle One:** Don't go to sleep angry.
    2. **Principle Two:** Guard yourself against the toxic waste of bitterness.
    3. **Principle Three:** If you have offended someone, quickly seek reconciliation.
    4. **Principle Four:** When insulted or mistreated, respond under control without escalating the conflict.
    5. **Principle Five:** Revenge is not sweet; don't taste it!
    6. **Principle Six:** Go the extra mile with people; don't make a federal case out of a misdemeanor.
    7. **Principle Seven:** Do all you can, but don't take responsibility for another's response.

STUDY OR DISCUSSION QUESTIONS

Part One
(60 minutes)

1. What are the greatest challenges you face in loving your "second family"?

2. What practical ideas for expressing love to co-workers can you add to those listed on page 120 of the chapter?

3. What would you say to Karen, the teacher in chapter 1, about how she should:

   resolve her own bitterness?

   treat her principal?

   pursue justice?

1. Share a conflict-ridden relationship with your discussion group as a case study for them to offer suggestions.

2. What do the following verses contribute to the study of anger? Proverbs 19:1; 19:19; 20:2; 22:24; 27:4; 30:33

3. What filters does God want us to put on our speech (Ephesians 4:29)?

4. What is a good example of a "federal" case in which a person should pursue justice through every legal and moral means possible?

OPTIONAL

Memorize Proverbs 16:32 and 1 Corinthians 13:1, 2.

— VIII

DIFFICULT
RELATIONSHIPS

*But I say to you, love your enemies and
pray for those who persecute you. . . .
For if you love those who love you, what
reward have you? Do not even the tax
gatherers do the same?*

MATTHEW 5:46

*Never pay back evil for evil to anyone. If
possible, so far as it depends on you, live
at peace with all men.*

ROMANS 12:17–18

A s you apply biblical principles to some of the really tough
issues of relationships, you will find help in this chapter in
dealing with vertical relationships and horizontal ones. Your superiors and subordinates make up your vertical relationships, and
your co-workers and clients make up the horizontal component.
Let's start with the one work relationship that is often a lightning
rod of contention: the difficult boss.

THE DIFFICULT BOSS

Over the last decade, I have addressed people around the country on honoring Christ in their work. In interaction with people during and after these seminars, I have heard some incredible and amazing stories of what management has done to people. We don't have time to discuss each one here, but I can propose that we look at the four most common problems people have shared with me and what the Scriptures have to say about them. Here are the four.

1. What do I do when I'm not appreciated for my contribution?

2. What do I do when I'm unfairly treated?

3. What do I do when I am given impossible job demands?

4. What do I do when double standards are applied?

Biblical Basics

The most critical point in dealing with a tough boss is to remember that *your real boss is Jesus Christ and that you should respect, honor, and obey your earthly boss as part of your Christ-following job description.* This is especially true if the boss is tough or unfair.

Second, you must remember that ultimately *God is in control of your circumstances and will only allow the boss to do that which He permits.* But with this concept, you should have a sense that God has placed this human boss in your life for a reason. It was not a divine mistake.

Third, *when you experience harshness or injustice, your model for how to respond is Jesus Christ.* Consider this crucial text.

> Servants, be submissive to your masters with all respect, not only to those who are good and gentle, but also to those who are unreasonable.
> For this finds favor, if for the sake of conscience toward God a man bears up under sorrows when suffering unjustly. For what credit is there if when you sin and are harshly treated, you

endure it with patience? But if when you do what is right and suffer for it you patiently endure it, this finds favor with God.

For you have been called for this very purpose, since Christ also suffered for you, leaving an example for you to follow in His steps. (1 Peter 2:18–21)

With these general ideas, let's look at some specifics.

When You Are Not Appreciated

As we have already seen, man cannot be depended on for appreciation. Your sense of appreciation must come from your Real Boss. But it is so human to want human approval and so natural to complain or be angry when we don't get what we think we deserve. But God has called us to live above this natural desire. It

---

"The more you look to man for glory and approval, the less you will look to Christ and vice versa."

---

is crucial that our motivation for work each day be to please Christ, not to impress man. If we do the latter, fine. But we should never come to expect it or need it.

If you find that your nose is out of joint because you're not being properly noticed, your pain may be allowed by God to help you purify your motive for work each day. You see, the more you look to man for glory and approval, the less you will look to Christ and vice versa. Jesus rebuked the Jews: "How can you believe, when you seek glory from one another, and do not seek the glory that is from the One and only God?" (John 5:44).

Paul went so far as to say that if he sought to please man, he would not be a follower of Jesus Christ (Galatians 1:10).

So if you are hurting or angry right now, take a moment to ask why. If you have been looking to man for glory, pause now and talk to God about it. Ask Him to give you a realistic view of man and to help you look to Him for approval and appreciation and to set you free from the need for human praise.

Perhaps God has called you to the situation you face to show the strength a Christ-follower can have who is not addicted to the glory of man.

When You Are Unfairly Treated

It happens. People I have talked to have lost careers and their entire life savings and have even been humiliated unfairly in front of others by their bosses. Needless to say, injustice is easier to identify than to respond to properly. The first question most Christians ask concerning their response is, "Must I always turn the other cheek?"

The answer is no, you do not always turn the other cheek and respond passively. The deciding issue is to ask what is at stake. If the unfair treatment is simply a minor embarrassment, forgive the offender and move on. If the problem threatens your ability to provide for yourself or your family, then you may want to take some measured steps to pursue justice.

The teacher who suffered an unfair evaluation from the principal could appeal it to the school board—not with anger or bitterness or revenge but just in pursuing justice. If she was embarrassed by a critical remark in the teachers lounge in front of her peers, she might want to let that small fish get away.

Jesus made a provocative statement when Peter brandished a sword in His defense: "Put your sword back into its place; for all those who take up the sword shall perish by the sword" (Matthew 26:52).

The point, of course, is that when you choose to respond actively and pursue justice, you enter a world of sword fighting. You could also get hurt. So before you file a grievance with your company, file a lawsuit, or take any other action, really pray about it, asking if this is a big issue worth going to war over or if it is small enough to let pass.

Practically speaking though, most of the injustices that people mention to me, require a passive response. Peter says, "Servants, be submissive to your masters with all respect, not only to those who are good and gentle, but also to those who are unreasonable" (1 Peter 2:18).

Regardless of how difficult the personality, how raspy the attitude, always show respect and honor. To do this you will need help from heaven. Every day ask God in prayer to allow you to love the offending person, to make a measured response, and to show respect. Don't join the coffee klatsch gripe sessions with co-workers. Take one day at a time.

Finally, accept God's leadership in your life for allowing the injustice to occur. God is not the author of evil, but He will permit it to occur if it achieves His higher purpose.

When You Have Impossible Job Demands

More and more impossible job demands are going to be an issue for people in companies that are being "thinned out" or "flattened."

This is tough, no question. All you can do is your best and do it with the best attitude you can muster. Here are some suggestions.

Remember the TRIALS acrostic? This is a great list of principles to review each day at work. If your job makes impossible demands, you especially will want to start each day with a spiritual orientation.

I have found that praying through each project and meeting before the day starts can make a big difference. Sometimes I have asked God to double my productivity and have seen Him do some amazing things!

Now, some people will waste time and energy complaining. But as the shoe commercial says, just do it!

Recognize that in every day there is just enough time to get done what God wants. So, assuming you were doing your part, if it didn't get done, there simply was not enough time. Your best is always enough.

Sometimes you can have some meaningful dialogue with the boss. Tell him or her you are very much interested in doing the best job you can but you seem to have too much responsibility; then ask the boss for suggestions. Another approach is to ask the boss to prioritize your projects for you in case you can't do them all. If you do this with a good attitude, you will likely have a good response.

Finally, I would urge you to be flexible on your hours. Some Christians think that a forty-hour workweek is found in the Bible somewhere and that it is a sin to work longer. Not so. The rhythm of life that God established was six days of work and rest on the seventh. In an agrarian environment this would be sunup to sundown.

So if the workweek for you over the next few years starts creeping up, be flexible. It looks as though businesses will need to thin out in the nineties. Be careful about drawing a line in the sand and saying you won't work longer than X hours per week. On the other hand, don't let work cost you your marriage or your family either. In a flexible response to excessive demands, "Let your forbearing spirit be known to all men. The Lord is near" (Philippians 4:5).

When Double Standards Are Applied

It doesn't seem fair. Something inside of you rejects the idea that managers expect things of you they don't do themselves. It is hypocritical and aggravating.

But it is in just such situations that you show what you really believe. First, it is clear that you must honor and respect your bosses and submit to them. If they say forty-five minutes for lunch and you see them taking two hours, you are still obligated to obey. Second, you must focus on *your attitude* and *not their behavior*. If you get angry, bad-mouth them behind their backs or become a complainer, then you have sunk to a level lower than those you are criticizing. You see, the most important response you can have to injustice is to have the right attitude. As followers of Christ we must expect injustice. We play the game of life differently and work by different rules than those who don't know Christ. A secular work world may get the best of us at times, but if we turn vindictive, arrogant, unsubmissive, angry, complaining—then we are the ones out of line.

Finally, accept the situation as a part of God's plan to help you learn Christlikeness. It is no accident that you are facing this situation. Accept His leadership in your life and make it a "win" for you.

When You Must Fire or Correct an Employee

I have never met a person in management who enjoyed this aspect of the job. I have had to do it and have felt the wave of nausea that comes with the task. Many believers struggle with such an unmerciful task. Many would say that they wait too long to correct or fire an employee.

How can we reconcile loving people with firing them? Where does turning the other cheek fit in?

To understand a biblical ethic concerning this issue, we must study what Jesus said in Matthew 23. In this vital passage, Jesus gives three essential aspects of relating to people. As you study these, you find a practical biblical ethic.

In verse 23, Jesus rebukes the religious leaders of the day for focusing on minors and missing majors. You see, they were very particular to give 10 percent of their spice racks, and yet they missed the most important aspect of the Law in relationships; namely justice, faithfulness, and mercy. These three principles of dealing with people God's way are worth a whole book in themselves. But for now imagine a triangle with each term at the corner.

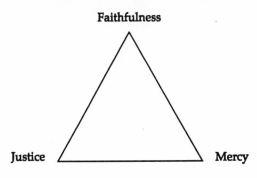

Faithfulness

Justice   Mercy

They form a triangle, because of a tension among them. For example, if you have an employee who steals from you, likely your response will focus on the justice side of the justice-mercy line. If you have a single parent whose child is sick and asks you for a sick day, you might be more merciful. Jesus had responses to people all across the justice-mercy continuum. This point is crucial because too many people think a Christian makes a milquetoast response to everything. Not true.

You see, it is unfair for one employee to sink the ship with a bad attitude or bad performance. It is also unfair to that person to shelter him from the consequences of his bad performance. It is also unfair to withhold feedback and correction from a person who is doing badly.

I can't make this task easy or fun. But I can say that while relationships are important, so is the work to be done. If your company has hired you to supervise, you owe it to everyone involved to be a caring boss with high standards, with clear direction to subordinates, and clear and fair consequences. Allowing sloppy work is not loving your people, it is not submission to your superiors, and it certainly does not provide the customer or end user with the best product or service.

THE DIFFICULT CO-WORKER OR CLIENT

It is important to recall all that has been said about loving your neighbor at work. Every day you are to move proactively to love the people you work with, even those who are difficult. Nothing is particularly impressive about loving those who are kind and grateful to you. But those difficult, insulting, arrogant, self-centered types—they are the ones who test our mettle. Jesus loves them and so should we.

Biblical Basics

Again, we should recall that these are people whom God has permitted into our "space" for a good reason. One worker who had this view was Joseph.

You remember the career path of this Old Testament hero. While he ended up second to Pharaoh, he started out being ejected from his family by his jealous brothers who sold him at an

---

"Nothing is particularly impressive about loving those who are kind and grateful to you. But those difficult, insulting, arrogant, self-centered types—they are the ones who test our mettle."

---

early age to slave traders. Because of their crime, Joseph had a very, very hard life. He went from being a son in a wealthy family to slavery and was subjected to a life of injustice.

Late in life Joseph ran into his slimy brothers who deserved to be slaughtered. What do you suppose Joseph said to them when he saw them after they came to beg for food in the court of Pharaoh, not knowing that they were in front of their brother? What would you have felt toward them? Joseph said this:

> And now do not be angry with yourselves, because you sold me here; for God sent me before you to preserve life. . . . Now therefore, it was not you who sent me here but God. . . . You meant evil against me, but God meant it for good in order to bring about this present result, to preserve many people alive. (Genesis 45:5–8; 50:20)

If we are going to talk biblical basics, we must underscore some vital principles that flow from this passage.

1. No matter what happens to you, no matter how meanly or unfairly you're treated, it can turn out for your ultimate good.

2. God is in full control of the events of your life and has a very good purpose for allowing difficulty, even if you can't see that purpose for years to come or at all in this life.

3. If you remain faithful to Him, God is the master of turning apparent disaster into unforeseen blessing and reward.

4. Joseph believed that his life had a high calling to serve God and people. This allowed him to accept God's hand in his life and to forgive his brothers for the evil they had committed.

I love this account of Joseph's life. But while we see his merciful response to his brothers and his forgiveness, we remember the justice-mercy continuum and recall that while our hearts must forgive, we may still have to pursue justice.

When Someone Doesn't Pay You

If there is a valid reason for not paying you, listen carefully. If there is no good reason, I recommend you take escalating steps to get your money. First, you might want to send a reminder in the mail. Then if there is no response, call. Then consider a collection agency or lawsuit. Nonpayment is serious and sets a precedent. Forgiving the debt may cost you much more than you think if word that you are soft leaks out.

Justice demands that you take steps to get the money.

When You Are Sued

If you are sued and the complaint is fair, try to settle out of court as soon as possible and reflect an attitude of regret.

If, however, you are unfairly sued, I suggest you play tough and fair. The football field is no place for a genteel approach. The players put their pads on for a benign battle. So is the legal system set up for aggressive opposition.

But again, guard your heart and review the biblical basics. Submit all you have to Christ and remind yourself that if He wants to take it away, fine. It is His anyway. This will keep you from letting the lawsuit dominate your existence. He is the One who provided what you have, and if it is taken, He can restore it or do something better.

When Someone Else Gets the Promotion You Deserved

This hurts. This hurts a lot! I would not tell you that you should not feel disappointed. You are only human.

But in your disappointment, remember that God is the author of all raises and promotions. "For not from the East or from the

---

"Often people at work thrive on a kind of low-voltage complaining and gossip that can sour the mood of even the most enthusiastic person."

West, nor from the desert comes exaltation; but God is the judge; He puts down one and exalts another" (Psalm 75:6–7).

A good test of your belief in this is the way you treat the one promoted. But don't forget what has been said about winning the praise of man and how fleeting it is. Also remember that from God's perspective if it had been in your best interest to get the promotion, you would have!

When the Coffee and the Conversation Are Bitter

When you are around people who have the flu, it is hard not to catch it! The same is true of complaining and gossip.

Often people at work thrive on a kind of low-voltage complaining and gossip that can sour the mood of even the most enthusiastic person. Self-centered people have nothing outside themselves to live for. Unlike you, they have nothing more than comfort and convenience to work toward; as we have already seen, their lives are filled with anger, fear, and emptiness.

It is easy to be caught off guard at informal discussion times and join in complaining and gossiping and showing a generally bad attitude. In the book of James the author suggests:

The tongue is a small part of the body, and yet it boasts of great things. Behold how great a forest is set aflame by such a small fire! And the tongue is a fire, the very world of iniquity; the tongue is set among its members as that which defiles the entire body and sets on fire the course of our life and is set on fire by hell. (James 3:5–6)

But most Christians I know understand all this and ask, "How can I avoid being like them?"

Let me suggest a starting point for you in being faithful to our Lord with your mouth and attitude at work.

1. Read the Bible every morning before work and look for some kind of application.

2. Study the passages that deal with your tongue (James 3; Ephesians 4:29; Philippians 2:14–15).

3. Consider the following rules:

   • Always be positive about others or don't say anything, unless a professional evaluation is required.

   • If others complain, it's probably better to just keep quiet.

   • Keep your guard up at lunch or other informal gatherings.

4. Pray about letting God put the right filters on your speech.

5. If you blow it today, tomorrow is a new day. We all blow it. Confess it to the Lord and work on it tomorrow.

6. Pray and pray and don't forget to pray!

When Others Are Slandering You

If someone formally says an untruth about you and it injures your ability to make an income, then you may want to talk to a lawyer. But sometimes rumors fly about people, and little people who want to appear important spread all sorts of criticism and comment. Such informal slander can really hurt.

Jack recently made regional manager for a sales company. Because he was not the senior candidate for the job, the grapevine put out the word that he got the promotion because he flattered the boss and was a "yes man" rather than for his hard work and dedication.

Jack's first impulse was to pull out some objective evidence of his hard work and achievement to silence the criticism. But the best way to silence such slander is to go to work for the right reasons and to do God's work in God's way. Slander and small people go together. You can never defend your character to the grapevine. God has to do it for you. The more you try to defend yourself in a situation like this, the more you will entrench in petty minds that the slander is true.

God is the One who establishes your reputation. Let Him unfold the truth about you as you do your work, not as you seek to defend yourself. If someone asks you a question, fine. But don't go to great lengths to correct misperceptions of you. Show them; don't tell them. Your conduct will speak louder and more forcefully. Don't worry about what man thinks of you!

WE ALL GO ON TO OUR REWARD

There is a very happy ending to this chapter. When you go to work tomorrow, think of yourself as receiving two paychecks—one now and one later. You can take this promise from God to the bank: for every time you do your work for Him, every time you maintain a good attitude toward difficult people, and every time you reflect Christlikeness, *you will be rewarded*. Christ offers a generous payment package. First, you may receive a promotion of some kind. But you can always count on an eternal reward in heaven.

The work world is filled with tension, injustice, and greed. You have been called to live above all of this and play the game by different rules. The people you have to feel sorry for are those who are not Christians. Those who are lost face uncertainty alone, have only themselves to live for, and feel dominated by selfish and egotistical values. We, on the other hand, get to live by a higher code, have more joy, and will be rewarded for our faithfulness no matter what happens in this life!

No real room for self-pity, is there?

REVIEW

Main Idea: You are responsible to have a Christ-like response to difficult people.

Key Points:

- Your real boss is Jesus Christ, and yet you should respect your earthly management.
- When you experience injustice, your model is Jesus Christ.
- Don't look for appreciation from people.
- If you do pursue justice for yourself, take measured steps.
- Justice and mercy must be balanced at work.
- No matter what happens or how unfairly they treat you, the situation can turn out for your good.
- God is in full control of your circumstances.
- God is the master of turning apparent disaster into unforeseen blessing and reward.
- Guard your tongue against bitterness, complaining, or gossip.

STUDY OR DISCUSSION QUESTIONS

1. How would you advise a friend who was bitter because he got little appreciation from his boss? Use the following outline for your thoughts:
   - What is his root problem?
   - What should he think about or consider?
   - What could he do?

2. Can you think of examples of injustice when a passive response was appropriate?

3. How about an incident when a "measured" response was appropriate?

4. How many work hours a week do you think are too many to keep life in balance?

5. When should a person consider leaving a job situation because of long hours?

6. Can you think of a bad situation that turned out for your ultimate good? What happened?

7. What would you do if someone did not pay you a large sum of money that you were owed?

8. When do you think criticism of another's job performance is appropriate? When is it not?

9. What do you think you should do if co-workers begin to criticize another worker in an informal situation?

— IX

CONQUERING
STRESS BEFORE IT
CONQUERS YOU

*Joe Pisciotto, chief of internal operations
at Crocker Anglo National Bank in San
Francisco, almost fainted one morning
when he entered his office. All twelve of
the girls who operate the complicated
banking machines had come to work in
maternity dresses—and the thought of
breaking in a dozen new employees at
once hit him like a sledge hammer. As he
was tottering near the window ledge, the
twelve girls chorused, "April Fool!"*

SAN FRANCISCO CHRONICLE

N ot Funny!
Stress and pressure are going to be a part of responsibility
and work. A certain amount of pressure can help us do our best
and work hard. But stress can be debilitating rather than motiva-
ting. It saps enjoyment of work and life and leaves us vulnerable,
not at full strength emotionally or even physically, just when our
best may be demanded of us.

THERE I WAS AT THIRTY THOUSAND FEET . . .

My first ride in the Air Force advanced jet trainer was a real thrill. The T-38 is a supersonic bird, a fighter pilot's equivalent of a sports car. It is fast, sleek, and maneuverable. Because it does not carry weapons or bombs, it is lighter and faster than many loaded fighters.

But picture the first ride in such a plane! The takeoff is much faster than you can imagine. You pass the one-thousand-foot marker on the runway in less than five seconds from brake release. Normal g forces for most acrobatic maneuvers are between four and five g's; i.e., while you are sailing around at five hundred miles an hour, your body weighs four to five times its normal weight.

On this first ride the instructor demonstrated a loop, a vertical circle in the sky that takes about ten thousand feet to accomplish. At the point in our circle when the aircraft was pointed straight up, with the sun in our faces, a red light suddenly glared at us from the dashboard. I was really scared. Why me? Why on my first ride?

The light on the dash spelled *fire*. Within eighteen inches of our fuel tank, a rubber bladder filled with four thousand pounds of JP-4, an explosive jet fuel, a temperature sensor picked up either a fire or an overheat situation. The instructor immediately shut the engine down, and we returned to base as fast as possible.

We did not worry about the fire warning light. We worried about a fire. The light was just a symptom of a deeper problem. Stress can be too.

In this chapter, I would like to address six major "fires" that create stress for people. There are others, but my experience has been that most stress comes from these six areas. The root causes of stress are the important ones.

Today there is ample material on stress management from secular seminars and self-help books. Unfortunately, most of the solutions to stress do not help solve the real causes of stress and offer only temporary help. I suppose that in the cockpit, I could have put a piece of paper over the light and not thought about it. I could have visualized a flower. I could have chanted a slogan or some Eastern religious saying. But the light was not the problem, and even

---

"The number one cause of stress is the wrong motivation for work: working to build your own ego or self-worth."

---

if I could have shifted my attention, it wouldn't have done any good. Please be wary of such stress management techniques.

As followers of Christ, we all sort of know that somehow Christ and His Word are the real answers to stress; we just don't know how. The starting point comes in knowing the root causes of stress and what the Bible says about them.

Let's launch into the first stress source.

EGO STRESS: GOING THE WRONG WAY ON A ONE-WAY STREET

The number one cause of stress is the wrong motivation for work: working to build your own ego or self-worth.

Most of us are not philosophers. We don't sit around and ask ourselves, "Why am I doing this project? What is my motive?" But a very real subterranean world in our minds includes motives and drives. We have already discussed this in chapter 3, but I would like to review this area quickly.

1. We go to work to bring glory to God, not ourselves.

2. We are just junior partners with God in our work, and our goal is to serve Him.

These truths speak volumes to our stress. Without a biblical framework for our work, we are doomed to a stress-filled life. We will sweat the small stuff and have little energy left over for the big stuff.

With an ego motivation, you will tend to envy the success of others. You will be frustrated and discouraged that others will not pay you the attention you think you deserve. You will find that the work world will not always cooperate with your goals and will keep you from attaining some illusory sense of "success." You will be gripped with the future, unable to rest and relax.

So how do you relieve ego stress? Here are some suggestions.

1. When you feel stress, ask yourself why. Why do I care so much about doing well?

2. Commit your work to Christ and ask Him to receive glory for the work you do.

3. Ask Him for help on whatever project you are working on.

4. Focus on doing your best, and leave the results to God. Give Him permission to let your project fail if that is His best for you and others.

5. Review the material on responsibility. Don't take more responsibility than you should.

Ego stress cannot be completely overcome with a simple prayer. Ego stress is like a Jack-in-the-box that pops back up after it has been pushed down.

Purifying your motivation for work takes daily maintenance. You must review God's Word on your work regularly. I suggest memorizing Scripture as a help. Bottom line: the more you see your work from God's perspective, the less stress you will have.

Now let's turn to another root cause of stress that is a twin sister to ego stress.

HOLDING ON TOO TIGHTLY

Please recall what has already been said about holding your career with a light touch. To do this you must learn to relax and trust God with the results of your work. Perhaps you are thinking, "That's fine, but God is not the one who will be fired or reprimanded if the project does not succeed!"

True, but so what if you don't have visible success? Will you be shot? Will they torture your family? How serious would it be?

What we really fear is insignificance or rejection. But painful as these feelings may be, the closer you get to Jesus Christ, the less success will mean to you.

You see, some of your needs can only be met in Christ. Some only can be met in human relationships. Some can only be met through creative expression. And some can only be met by your own efforts. Surely work is important and necessary for possessions. But it can never define your worth as a person. It can never fulfill the needs that a close family or friendship can bring.

A friend of mine recently recounted a conversation with a woman dying of cancer. Bob asked her what it was that she was learning about life from her situation. She said that she was learning what it is hard to say goodbye to. Clothes, furniture, cars were very easy to say goodbye to. It was much harder to bid farewell to her children, husband, and close friends. Perhaps people learn more about life on the eve of death than at any other time.

Please don't get me wrong—work is important, and your work really matters to God. But if you are holding on too tightly, it may be a symptom that you are looking to work to meet the needs that only Christ can fill or that intimate relationships were designed to fill.

For more on sweating the big stuff, read *How to Succeed Where It Really Counts* (by Doug Sherman and Bill Hendricks, Colorado Springs, CO: NavPress, 1989).

TIME AND RESPONSIBILITY STRESS

Sarah is a capable woman in her mid-forties. She is an accountant and the Chief Financial Officer of a medium-sized insurance company. She is married and has two children ages ten and sixteen. She appears to have it all. She makes a good income, enjoys the status of her job, and holds down the fort on the home front as a wife and mother. Her husband flies for a major airline, and they get free passes to anywhere in the world. He also sells real estate when he's not flying. They attend a fine church, and their kids are very active in the youth program.

But Sarah is miserable. She feels she is in a vise that grips her more tightly every day. Executive responsibility is all-consuming. Problems often need to be solved immediately, schedules must be met, and meetings often go overtime. The phone never stops ringing with people wanting her advice, her approval, or her attention.

At home she faces similar demands that are never satisfied. The kids like to be involved in sports and after-school activities. This requires a different schedule each day. Her husband helps when he is in town, but he is usually gone two weeks of the month. While they get the free airline passes, they never have time to use them.

Worst of all, Sarah sees no end in sight. Her schedule tends to exhaust her, leaving her on edge in the evenings. But she doesn't want to be this way. In fact, she lives with severe guilt over this. She loves her career, and she loves her family and wants to do a good job in both. But she feels that the demands of life are crushing her, sapping all enjoyment of these two areas.

You don't have to be an executive to feel this kind of stress. If you supervise a company or a household or just work long hours, you can feel it. Commonly, people feel so spent they can't do a good job in any area of life. But as soon as one area suffers, the overall stress load increases.

This kind of stress is mostly generated from outside pressures. As companies "thin out" and "flatten," people will be doing more than one job. Managers will have a wider span of control too—greater responsibility and more to worry about. So the outlook for this kind of stress is not good.

So what do you do? The most important suggestion I could give you is to suggest that you get a day to yourself and get your life organized. Most will people organize work areas and let chaos ruin nonwork areas. But if chaos invades nonwork areas, there will be chaos at work too.

In *How to Balance Competing Time Demands*, I propose that life can be divided into five main areas: work, family, personal life, church life, and community life. These five areas make up a kind of pentathlon. Like the athletic pentathlon, the Christian life in-

---

"One of the greatest dangers today is to pour all of your emotional energy into work."

---

volves doing all aspects well. But to do this we must move deliberately in all areas, particularly the nonwork areas. One of the greatest dangers today is to pour all of your emotional energy into work, leaving little for nonwork areas. But it takes as much energy and effort to have a good marriage, be a good parent, grow in Christ, and help others as it does to have a good career. Setting goals in each area can be a great help to bringing balance in your life. (For more on how to set goals and creatively put balance in your life, see *How to Balance Competing Time Demands*, Doug Sherman and Bill Hendricks, Colorado Springs, CO: 1989.)

Think of your time as you would a budget. You have a limited amount of time, and the amount you give to each category must be limited too. You must accept tradeoffs, which is very hard for people like Sarah to do. She has a mental image of a perfect executive, a perfect mother, a perfect wife, a perfect Christian worker, and a perfect citizen, but she cannot do it all. She cannot perfectly meet all the needs. She must have a measure of success and accept that God will make up what is missing. She may not get to make every sports activity the kids are in. She may not be able to answer every question or take every project on at work. She may have to maximize the time she has with her husband and accept its brevity. But sanity can be brought to a situation like this only if she considers how her whole life can be managed and prays through the tradeoffs.

This is hard for me personally. I want to save the world. But last time I checked, heaven was not taking applications for this job. Jesus Christ pretty well has a lock on this task. What I need to do is to have a measure of faithfulness to God in all areas of my life.

One source of stress is simply poor management of the workday. While this section is not designed to be a comprehensive program of time management, three lessons on the subject can be drawn from the Bible. The first is from a grape farmer. The following passage tells a story with a significant lesson on our work habits.

> I passed by the field of the sluggard,
> And by the vineyard of a man lacking sense;
> And behold, it was completely overgrown
>   with thistles,
> Its surface was covered with nettles,
> And its stone wall was broken down.
> When I saw, I reflected on it;
> I looked and received instruction.
> A little sleep, a little slumber,
> A little folding of the hands to rest.
> Then your poverty will come as a robber,
> And your want like an armed man.
> (Proverbs 24:30–34)

Let's look at this closely. First we see the author walking by a field and drawing a lesson from what he sees. It's a vineyard, a farm that requires a lot of maintenance and work. But the field shows signs of neglect. There are weeds, thistles, and nettles. The stone wall protecting the vineyard from the animals that like the fruit of the vine is in disrepair. The caretaker has not kept up the work.

As the speaker reflects on the situation, he lingers on two sayings: "a little sleep" and "a little folding of the hands to rest." Nothing wrong with either sleep or relaxing, but here the farmer is procrastinating: "Maybe I'll just relax now. I'll get to the work tomorrow." It is a classic approach to work we don't like to do or that has less appeal than other activities.

But the result of procrastination is much worse than you would think. The result is like the disaster of being robbed by an armed man. Just as no one schedules a robber on the calendar, so the disaster will come suddenly and unexpectedly. The point is this: procrastination is the path to sudden and unexpected disaster.

Have you ever seen the look on people's faces when the TV shows them mobbing the post office at eleven-thirty on April 15, trying to get a postmark before midnight? Stress wrinkles show on cheeks, tense and nervous drivers honk, a wave of nausea moves over the entire crowd. Not a pretty picture. What happens when you don't return a phone message that you prefer not making? What happens when you put off a project you don't like till the last possible moment and then your schedule is interrupted? Stress, stress, and more stress.

Perhaps it is important to identify the projects you least like to work on and do them first. Return the phone messages you don't want to do first.

Sometimes deadlines are missed. But when they are missed because we have procrastinated, we feel pretty bad.

A second lesson from Proverbs comes from an insect, the ant. While not a friend at the family picnic, she makes a fine professor of good work habits.

> Go to the ant, O sluggard,
> Observe her ways and be wise,
> Which having no chief officer or ruler,
> Prepares her food in the summer,
> And gathers her provision in the harvest.
>
> (Proverbs 6:6–8)

The ant is self-motivated and plans ahead. If she does not, she will not survive. How about you? Do you plan out each day? Do you set goals and think through how you can maximize your time and effort? Organization and planning are biblical values and necessary components of doing your work well.

The passage also implies a third lesson: prioritizing.

Today, being busy is no virtue. I once had a student pilot who got lost over El Paso. As we cruised along at 550 miles per hour, he said to me, "Sir, I don't know where we're going, but we're making good time."

The challenge of work today is figuring out the right heading and staying on course. In every job, there are crucial projects, important projects, and nice-to-do projects. The time you spend assigning priorities will save you three times that amount of time in execution. Like flying an airplane—there is no advantage to going fast if you are going in the wrong direction!

By not prioritizing your work, you are inviting stress into your life.

OWING A DEBT TO SOCIETY

Bob and Jane fell in love with a two-story colonial home near Washington, D.C. Knowing they would fall in love with it even though it cost more than they wanted to spend, the realtor wisely showed them this home. Bob turned to Jane and said that even though the payments were very high, he thought they could swing it.

And in reality they could *if:*

- He kept his job and got yearly raises,
- She kept her job, even if they had children,
- No one had major medical bills,
- Inflation did not exceed his pay increases,
- No major change in expenses occurred,
- They only sneezed on alternate Wednesdays.

I'm sure you get the idea. Debt and stress are best of friends. And they're both related to ego. Ego, stress, and debt are profoundly connected. Let me explain.

Ego tempts us to presume on the future, to presume that we will beat the odds that forecast interruptions in income, deterioration of our health, and other downturns. Ego also echoes the hair commercial: "It may cost more, but I'm worth it." The back side of this comment involves self-pity when we can't have what we

---

"Debt and stress are best of friends. And they're both related to ego."

---

want. Ego can tempt you to imprudent financial debt service that will stress you *when:*

- You lose your job,
- Pay raises don't come,
- Jane wants to stay at home when little Arthur is born,
- Your mother needs financial help for a hip-replacement,
- An oil crisis in the Middle East doubles inflation,
- Your car needs both a new engine and an exorcism.

The unexpected will happen. So should we not have any debt at all? This is not my point. The ball is in your court to seek the Lord and His wisdom in prudent financial moves. But be careful with debt. Like fire, it has a good use, but it also can burn you! Mistakes made in the area of debt, whether they be credit card, mortgage, or business debt, may take years to correct. Please be careful.

WHEN YOUR TANK IS ON EMPTY

Recently I was with a friend in Boston. Bob is a very successful businessman and a dedicated Christian. While we were driving along the Charles River, I noticed the fuel indicator, a habit, I suppose, from my flying days. The needle was to the left of empty. We had to have used up most of the fumes in the tank. So I said "Bob, what a nice car! How does it drive on empty?" Bob said, "Great! I'll steer and you push. It will work fine!" People, like cars, don't work well when their emotional tanks or physical tanks are empty.

Think back to Sarah's situation. She is running on fumes. She is worn out, both physically and emotionally. Often in this situation people think they can microwave themselves with a short intense vacation to restore the tanks. Sometimes this works. Travel agents will tell you, though, that a fourth of those who travel abroad on vacations get sick. Sometimes just knowing that the work is piling up while you're gone can ruin even the nicest vacation. And frankly, the phrase "family vacations" can be an oxymoron. The kids fight; they need continual stimulation and entertainment. Often the romantic notion of a family vacation turns into an intense relational experience that leaves everyone at odds with each other.

So what is the answer? In part, life management is at stake, which is why I am urging you to go through the recommended study of *How to Balance Competing Time Demands*. But I want to highlight here two needs often overlooked.

Think back to *The Ten Commandments*. You remember— Charlton Heston and those big tablets. Maybe you read the book instead.

The fourth commandment says this:

> Remember the sabbath to keep it Holy. Six days you shall labor and do all your work, but the seventh day is a sabbath of the Lord your God; in it you shall not do any work, you or your son or your daughter, your male or your female servant or your cattle or your sojourner who stays with you. For in six days the Lord made the heavens and the earth, the sea and all that is in them, and rested on the seventh day; therefore the Lord has blessed the sabbath day and made it holy. (Exodus 20:8–11)

There were good reasons for this law. First, the God who made you and me designed us for a rhythm of life that included one day a week for rest. Without this rest, life becomes dull and dreary. Now, rest might involve activity, but it is clearly a break from work responsibilities.

Second, it was an opportunity for Israel to trust God to meet their needs even though they were not working. You see, in farming the work is never done. They had to relax even with seed to

---

"It would be wrong not to plan for rest, recreation, and a time to refocus on God."

---

sow or crops to harvest, and they had to trust that if they obeyed God, He would make up what they lost in their day of rest.

Third, the Sabbath provided a time to refocus and renew their relationship with God.

Now the big question: Is the sabbath law in effect today? My study says that it is not in force today in the specific way it was for Israel. But the basic idea behind it is. So, no, it is not a sin to go to work on Sunday as a nurse. But it would be wrong not to plan for rest, recreation, and a time to refocus on God. Your tank will quickly drop to empty. You may function for a while without such rest, but you are working on borrowed time if you do. Then don't be too surprised if a vacation still doesn't meet your needs. The Sabbath is a weekly program, not two weeks a year at Wally World.

The second need we all have is to build a scaffolding of friends around us. You see, work is only good for meeting your creative expression needs. But your emotional tank needs the filling that you will receive from friends. They are a part of God's provision for your happiness.

But I hear from some that they would *love* to have the time for rest and friends, but they just can't. I'm sure this is true for a few of us. I used the same argument myself, so I am acquainted with it. But often, it feels good to be needed so much. The PTA, the soccer league, the church finance committee, the boss needs your help, and on and on.

But an empty tank leads to a miserable life and weak relationships with short fuses and little love. We become like porcupines that are okay as long as you don't get close.

Sometimes, it takes real discipline to limit our activities to make time to get our tanks filled. But remember, procrastination is the path to sudden and unexpected disaster!

STRESSED FOR SUCCESS

Stress will probably be a disease on the rise throughout this decade. Right motives and expectations are critical to the cure. A balanced life and good work habits are just as important.

God designed work for us to enjoy. Conflicts and stress can sap the life out of this joy. But there is hope if you know the source of these problems and have God's perspective on what to do about them.

Imagine receiving a letter in the mail from Jesus Christ.

Dear Son or Daughter,

I know that you are tense and nervous, that you are worried about the success of your work, and that it has a grip on you. You feel your shoulders have more weight on them than you can carry.

Because I love you so much, because I hurt when you hurt, I want to remind you of My truth and My ways of dealing with My children.

You should remember that your work matters to Me. I care about your projects, your meetings, your success. After all, you are working for Me. We are partners. But you are My junior partner in all you do. My shoulders are broad enough for the responsibility. Yours are not. Without My help, you can do nothing. With My help, you can accomplish exactly what I want.

Much of your fear is the fear of failing before others. It is pride. Your stress simply allows you to see how much you care for the glory of man.

I want you to feel My presence with you. I want you to trust Me for the results of your work. Relax, work hard, and enjoy it;

but trust Me. See success not in goal achievement, but in pleasing Me today with your work.

I love you so much, and remember, your work matters to Me.

Your Lord and Friend,
Jesus Christ

Because God wants you to enjoy your work fully, the entire next chapter is devoted to helping you put more joy in it.

REVIEW

Main Idea: Stress is often the symptom of a deeper problem.

Key Points:

- A major source of stress is an ego motivation for work.
- A major source of stress comes from holding too tight a grip on the results of our work.
- A major source of stress is the lack of life planning.
- A major source of stress is too much debt.
- A major source of stress is empty physical and emotional tanks.

STUDY OR DISCUSSION QUESTIONS

1. Rank order the following sources of stress you experience. The number *1* means the biggest source; *5*, the smallest. You most often face:

   ☐ stress from wrong motivation

   ☐ stress from holding on too tightly

   ☐ stress from poor work habits

☐ stress from debt

☐ stress from physical and emotional fatigue

2. What could you do to have more of a God-centered motivation for work?

3. What advice would you give Sarah?

4. How much do you think nonwork responsibilities affect work stress? Why?

5. What are some common work habits that could reduce stress for you?

6. List four principles related to debt that you could use to teach teenagers to avoid getting in over their heads when they become adults?

7. What things do you do to have regular rest and recreation?

8. What are your views on the Sabbath? Is the commandment applicable today, and what does it mean?

9. Which parts of the TRIALS acrostic are most helpful in dealing with stress? Explain.

10. Reflect on these passages:
    • Philippians 4:6–7
    • 1 Peter 5:7
    • Matthew 6:25–33

— X

REALLY ENJOYING YOUR WORK

Here is what I have seen to be good and fitting: to eat, to drink and enjoy oneself in all one's labor in which he toils under the sun during the few years of his life which God has given him; for this is his reward.

ECCLESIASTES 5:18

I nteresting, isn't it, that the Scriptures refer to joy as a choice? It is commanded, "Finally my brethren, rejoice in the Lord" (Philippians 3:1). Joy is considered a result of obeying the Holy Spirit: "But the fruit of the Spirit is love, joy. . ." (Galatians 5:22). In difficulty we are to consider our circumstances a net gain of joy: "Consider it all joy my brethren when you encounter various trials. . ." (James 1:2–4).

CHOICES

Apparently, joy is both an emotion and a decision. Parents see this easily with their kids. After a day of shopping for clothes, a teenager may explode when a particular item is not purchased. Instead of choosing to think about what she did get, she focuses on what she did not. Her anger is a choice; so, too, would be her joy.

A husband who has lost a wife may have joy in the midst of grief and loss. The joy can come from the celebration of the time they had together, of their ultimate reunion in heaven, and of God's unseen plan, which permitted her departure. The grief lingers but will fade in time. In contrast, the joy can grow.

Now there is no question that emotions have a mind of their own and do not always follow our commands. But two loyal parts of our selves will obey when we say jump: our bodies and our minds.

While you may not be in full control of your feelings, you can decide what you are to think about and what you do. And right thinking and right decisions tend in time to pull the emotions along with them. But the starting point has to do with our minds and our bodies.

Happiness is a choice. In part, it is the result of what we choose to do and what we choose to think about. However, we tend to approach life otherwise. Our tendency is to feel that we are the victims of our circumstances and that our emotions can only follow the quality of our circumstances.

Think of the familiar expression, "You made me mad!" Is it true? No. I can choose to be mad or not, but you cannot make me mad. Being mad may be quite understandable. But it is not demanded.

But while this is true, there are some laws of gravity that impact our feelings. If you don't sleep, you will feel tired. If you smoke, you will likely get cancer and not feel too good.

When it comes to your attitude and feelings about your work, two major points follow from all that has been said.

1. Your enjoyment of work is in large part a matter of choice, especially concerning what you think and do.

2. You must follow certain laws to enjoy work fully.

With these points in mind, let's look at five prerequisites to enjoying your work fully.

TO ENJOY YOUR WORK FULLY, YOU MUST ENJOY THE LORD

The wisest man on earth penned this requisite. It is incredibly profound. If you get only this idea from this book, you will have the most important principle. Please notice that it does not say that to enjoy your work you must believe in Christ and be born again. I assume you have already done that and that you are well

---

"The path to really enjoying your job is to have a warm personal relationship with your Lord and Savior and to make Him the controlling center of each workday."

---

aware that just knowing Christ in a vague or distant way is no promise of happiness on the job. In fact, many Christians carry the sorriest attitude about their work.

The expression is not that to enjoy your work you should belong to the right church or believe the right doctrine. It simply says that the path to really enjoying your job is to have a warm personal relationship with your Lord and Savior and to make Him the controlling center of each workday.

Drift with me for a moment, though, down a path of imagining what work would be like without an intimate relationship with God.

At least twelve terrible consequences are in store for any person, Christian or not, who checks God at the door of his office.

1. Without God's perspective on work, work has no ultimate meaning or purpose.

2. Without God's approval and His view of our worth, we are doomed to derive our self-esteem from a fickle crowd of people whose applause never lasts long.

3. Without God's purpose in work, people are left with an addiction to ego biscuits—competition, consumption, and competence.

4. Without the belief that a good God is in control of our lives, we would be left feeling that we are just victims.

5. Without the belief in God, we would have no sense of ultimate justice. Thus, if there is no justice now, there is no justice.

6. Without an intimate relationship with God, there would be no one to relate to throughout the day. There would be no one to thank.

7. Without God's view of our worth, we are left insecure trying to prove our worth. Our sense of significance is on the line every day.

8. Without a sense that God is in control, all celebration is in the shadow of ominous uncertainty.

9. Without God's wisdom applied to daily work problems we must look to ourselves for insight and direction or follow the prevailing course of secular thought for daily decisions and problem solving.

10. Without God's empowering, there is no real hope for our character to change.

11. Without God's help, we would not recognize what Rudyard Kipling called the two great impostors: success and failure.

12. Without God's forgiveness, what would you do with guilt?

King Solomon set out on a course to work and live without reference to God at all. He concluded that without God in the picture, work is empty: "Thus I considered all my activities which my hands had done and the labor which I had exerted, and behold all was vanity and striving after wind and there was no profit under the sun" (Ecclesiastes 2:11).

> **"Where is your relationship with Christ today? This is the most profound question you could ever ask another human being."**

Is it not relatively apparent that without His help, His wisdom, His perspective, His supernatural help, work will be empty and futile?

Your joy at work is directly tied to your involving God in the day-to-day issues and decisions and to your applying a biblical view to your work.

So what would a God-centered day at work look like?

Well, intimacy with Christ is more easily recognized than described. But the word *intimacy* is a good place to start.

Many today, I feel, have a principle-oriented relationship with Christ. They know facts about Christ and would do well on a multiple choice test concerning who He is. But they do not know Him.

Imagine that near where you are right now there is a room. In this room is a large overstuffed chair, and sitting in that chair is Jesus Christ. You immediately feel the power of His presence as you enter the room. But it is not scary at all. In fact it is peaceful. Now imagine His face and those deep, dark eyes that can look right through you and know everything you have ever thought or said. Then there are those scars on His face and hands.

What would you say to Him? What would He say to you?

Would you hesitate uneasily, almost waiting for an introduction? Would you fall at His feet in the presence of both your king and your best friend?

Where is your relationship with Christ today? This is the most profound question you could ever ask another human being.

You see, experiencing Christ throughout your day involves communion with this person. It involves spending time listening to Him speak to you through His Word and your conscience. Can you think of something you have read from the Bible recently that has really stood out to you as though God were highlighting it for you personally?

Jesus is by nature a communicator. He wants to speak to you and wants you to talk to Him. People who spend time with Christ daily are noticeably different. They have a winsomeness about them. You can tell when a person knows the face of Christ.

Now please know that I am talking about more than just reading the Bible, although Bible reading is certainly included. You see it is possible just to read the Scriptures and never make contact with the author of the Scriptures. Dr. A. W. Tozer has said,

> For it is not mere words that nourish the soul, but God Himself, and unless and until the hearers find God in personal experience they are not the better for having heard the truth. The Bible is not an end in itself, but a means to bring men to an intimate and satisfying knowledge of God, that they may enter into Him, that they may delight in His Presence, may taste and know the inner sweetness of the very God Himself in the core and center of their hearts. (*Pursuit of God,* A. W. Tozer, Wheaton, Ill: Tyndale House Publishers, 9–10)

This is what I want for you and me—to sense the divine presence every day of our lives, to hear His voice and to obey His Word progressively! So how do you really get to know Christ in this way? Let me offer some first steps.

1. Begin reading the Scriptures, taking one chapter or less each day. The book of John is an excellent place to start. As you read, realize that Christ is the central theme of both testaments and begin getting to know Him.

2. Look each day for a new thought about God, a new thought about yourself, or an idea you can apply in your behavior.

3. Work at taking time during your workday to talk to Him. It doesn't have to be long, but the time you spend will be important. Hopefully this will eventually become a natural part of your day.

4. Regularly review three questions in your mind:
   - Lord, what would You have me do?
   - Lord, what attitude would You have me maintain?
   - Lord, how would You have me respond to this person or situation?

A close relationship with Christ will bring you a lot of joy. It will greatly enhance your enjoyment of your work too.

"Careers rise and fall. If you don't have an enduring relationship with Christ when you crash, you will crash hard."

The greatest tragedy I have seen has been life crashing in on a person who really has only a career in life. Careers rise and fall. If you don't have an enduring relationship with Christ when you crash, you will crash hard. The person who knows Christ may crash, but will walk away.

TO ENJOY YOUR WORK, YOU MUST HAVE A COMPELLING VISION OF WHAT YOU DO AND WHY YOU DO IT

Ever lose the forest for the trees? One night I was in a survival training course in the mountains of Colorado. This course was given to all Air Force Academy freshman cadets to prepare us in case one day we were shot down and had to escape enemy ground forces.

One night a few of my classmates were walking around in thirty-five-degree weather, with rain pouring down. The question that confronted us was, "Why am I going through this?" At the time we were miserable. The compelling notion before us, though, was that we were preparing to serve our country.

A Christian's motivation is even better—serving the Ruler of the kings of the earth. Without such a compelling vision we would have quit.

There is a parallel. You will burn out on just going to work to get a paycheck, to buy more food, to have the energy to go to work. Please recall that your purpose is to bring glory to God. You are also to serve others and to be the hands of Christ. Like Christ, you are a servant to the needs of those around you.

You need an inner sense that you are doing what God has called you to do. Perhaps it is clear to you that He led you to this job. Perhaps your conscience reinforces this and tells you that you are in the right place with the responsibilities He has given you.

All of the above should give you a sense of destiny. Certainly all work has its limits. Very few, if any, of us will change the world. But that is not the goal. The goal is to please Jesus Christ each day and to do what He wants. That is real glory!

TO ENJOY YOUR WORK, YOU MUST BE REALISTIC ABOUT THE FACT THAT YOU ARE NOT GOING TO CHANGE THE WORLD

It is important to join the fight against all that is wrong in the world. It is important to try to help your company be as ethical as it can. But realize that in this life, the world will never be ideal: "What is crooked cannot be straightened, and what is lacking cannot be counted" (Ecclesiastes 1:15). It is enough to think of changing your corner of the world. But as someone once said, I would rather fail in a cause that will ultimately succeed than succeed in a cause that will ultimately fail. Justice will some day come, all evil will be quarantined to a part of the universe, and the faithful will reign with God in glory!

TO ENJOY YOUR WORK, YOU MUST BE REALISTIC ABOUT WORK AND THE FRUIT OF YOUR WORK

Your possessions meet some needs for you. Your work meets some needs for you. Relationships with people meet some needs for you, and God meets some needs for you. As I mentioned earlier, a screwdriver is good but not for eye surgery. Work has great value, but it cannot meet all of your needs. It is important that we set realistic expectations; otherwise we will be set up for great disappointment.

Much has been written about the unrealistic expectations of the baby boom generation. Daniel Yankelovich in *New Rules*, contrasts the expectations of this generation and their parents. For the parents he writes.

Success meant being good parents—

- "Providing for the family"
- "Making a home for the children"
- "Having a stable family"
- "Giving the children the maximum you could give them—mostly material things"
- "Giving kids the chance they didn't have"

Success meant money—getting it, holding onto it, buying things with it.

Success meant social standing and respectability.
(*New Rules: Searching for Self-fulfillment in a World Turned Upside Down*, New York: Bantam, 1982, 110)

But the baby boom group wants and expects much, much more: "creativity, leisure, autonomy, pleasure participation, community, adventure, vitality, stimulation, tender-loving care. . . . They seek to satisfy both the body and spirit which is asking a great deal of the human condition" (p. 8). The idea here is that baby boomers may be expecting way too much of a work world that has been cursed as a result of sin:

> Cursed is the ground because of you;
> In toil you shall eat of it all the days of your life.
> Both thorns and thistles it shall grow for you,
> And you shall eat the plants of the field;
> By the sweat of your face you shall eat bread,
> Till you return to the ground,
> Because from the dust you were taken
> And to the dust you shall return.
> (Genesis 3:17b–19)

The nature of the work world is often two steps forward and one back. It is often frustrating and difficult as I am sure you know. But a realistic assessment of the nature of work can lead us back to the fact that to enjoy our work, we must keep Christ at the center of each workday. Otherwise our happiness will be based on the circumstances of the difficult work world, with its injustice and its normal operating procedure of two steps forward and one back.

TO ENJOY YOUR WORK, YOU MUST BE REALISTIC ABOUT THE LENGTH OF YOUR LIFE

Boston is a wonderful town full of America's history. Downtown, there is a church built before the Revolutionary War. Outside the church is a cemetery where many of the signers of the Declaration of Independence were buried. On one of the tombstones the following epitaph is written:

> Stop here my friend and cast an eye.
> As you are now, so once was I.
> As I am now, so you must be.
> Prepare for death and follow me.

The prospect of death for followers of Christ is sobering, but it helps to bring into focus how we should live our lives. Those who know they have only a short time to live often have the healthiest perspective on life. We are told in Scripture to have this perspective: "As he had come naked from his mother's womb, so will he return as he came. He will take nothing from the fruit of

---

"The prospect of death for followers of Christ is sobering, but it helps to bring into focus how we should live our lives."

---

his labor that he can carry in his hand" (Ecclesiastes 5:15). This view will help us to enjoy life more and take seriously only those things that should be taken seriously.

Live life and enjoy it. Give priority to what you can take with you.

TO ENJOY YOUR WORK, YOU MUST BE REALISTIC ABOUT YOUR SHORTCOMINGS

I hope you can laugh about your weaknesses. If you cannot, it is no laughing matter because "indeed there is not a righteous man on earth who continually does good and who never sins" (Ecclesiastes 7:20).

The point is not to be nonchalant that we won't ever be perfect, or to pursue spiritual mediocrity, but to accept that we are human. As humans we need the Savior. Knowing that we will not be perfect can help us to accept that in this life *progress* is all we can really hope for.

So to enjoy your work fully, you must be realistic about it and the fruits of work. Just as when you eat a meal you don't expect that you will never be hungry again, don't be unrealistic about work. Don't let your life lean on a table with wobbly legs.

TO ENJOY YOUR WORK, YOU MUST WORK ON A POSITIVE ATTITUDE

In large part this whole book has been written to help you in this area. Take a moment to ask yourself what attitude you would like to have toward your work. What attitude would God want you to have?

The Bible urges us to approach our work with enthusiasm, with gratitude that we have a job, with a sense of adventure, and with joy.

People depend on you to have a good attitude because good work usually follows from a good attitude. But remember, the right attitude comes from right thinking and right actions. To have enthusiasm, you must frame your perspective around God's ideas of work.

Think back to the ideas of previous chapters. So far you have been encouraged to think about:

- right motives
- making Christ the center of each workday
- seeing your work as a schoolhouse for learning Christlikeness
- genuine love for your co-workers
- your significance in Christ

Imagine that you reflected on some of these ideas and attendant Scriptures each workday. Do you think that would make a difference in your attitude? A positive attitude comes from making Christ the center of each workday and thinking about His truths relative to your work. You can't always control your attitude or feelings, but you can control your thoughts and your actions. Study these key passages regularly: Ephesians 6:5–8; Colossians 3:22–24; Psalm 8; Ecclesiastes 5:18.

The second feature of your attitude is gratitude. Much has been said in chapter 6 about being thankful for what you have rather than complaining about what you lack.

A friend of mine is a surgeon who operates on patients with life-threatening problems. Imagine what the day is like for him.

> *"The Bible urges us to approach our work with enthusiasm, with gratitude that we have a job, with a sense of adventure, and with joy."*

Dealing with tense, nervous patients and family in "pre-op," co-ordinating the surgical team that is sober with the life-and-death struggle on the table, then facing the family when the operation is a success—or a failure. When he walks through the door to his house, he faces kids and a wife. When they get sick with colds and flu, he finds it incredibly hard to feel sympathy for them. Their problem seems so trivial.

We need sometimes to get perspective on what is trivial and what is not in our work. When the temperature of the coffee is tepid . . .

Have you ever talked to a person who is out of work? How about to a sole wage earner who has just been laid off and has a high mortgage to pay? These situations should make us stop to think before we complain.

A third dimension of maintaining a positive attitude involves a daily housecleaning of bad thoughts and attitudes, the little demons that torment you and affect others. To clean them out, first admit them and agree with God that they are bad. Second, pray and ask for God's help in overcoming them. Third, review God's truth that opposes them. His Word can have a powerful impact on your life! Here are some of the bad attitudes mentioned so far in this book.

- anger
- complaining
- envy
- fear of insignificance
- fear of the future
- fear of rejection
- revenge
- self-hate

All of these and other bad attitudes must be dealt with if you are going to enjoy your work.

Finally, there is one more requisite to enjoying your work.

TO ENJOY YOUR WORK, YOU MUST CELEBRATE LIFE AND ENJOY FAMILY AND FRIENDS

If you are a teetotaling evangelical who disdains alcohol and drunkenness, then you can actually learn something from the "Miller Time." There is a real place for celebration in life. God wants you to savor life, to live it to the full. Granted, drunkenness is hardly the way to do it. But being too busy to enjoy a park, the mountains, or some good exercise is not good either. Parties with friends are great opportunities to celebrate. Solomon urges us: "Go then, eat your bread in happiness, and drink your wine with a cheerful heart; for God has already approved your works. Let your clothes be white all the time [i.e., regularly be in a mood of celebration] and let not oil be lacking on your head" (Ecclesiastes 9:7–8).

At your desk you may want to pause and just celebrate that you are alive! That you have friends and family! Taking a few moments to savor what God has given you and to thank Him can be wonderful.

Life as God designed it for you and me is to include celebration. So "party hearty"—in an appropriate way, of course.

Really Enjoying Your Work

With celebration, really enjoy friends and family. If you don't, work will be boring. A good check on how you are doing is how much emotional energy you have left for nonwork aspects of your life. If 90 percent of your emotional energy is put into work, you will soon become an unhappy person. Solomon suggests this: "Enjoy life with the woman whom you love all the days of your fleeting life which he has given to you under the sun; for this is your reward in life, and in your toil in which you have labored under the sun" (Ecclesiastes 9:9).

What is your reward in the midst of the toil of work? It is relationships, enjoying life with someone you love. May God help us both suck the marrow out of life and celebrate all that He has given us!

A CHANGE IN CIRCUMSTANCE OR A CHANGE IN ATTITUDE?

This chapter has dealt with the attitude change. Surely, some of us need to change jobs. But the job God has given to you is a gift. Our attitude toward this job is in large measure a choice of what we think about and how we act: "Finally, brethren whatever is true, whatever is honorable, whatever is right, whatever is pure, whatever is lovely, whatever is of good repute, if there is any excellence and anything worthy of praise, let your minds dwell on these things" (Philippians 4:8). We are not victims when it comes to our attitudes. We have in the Bible God's blueprint for lives that will bring us joy.

REVIEW

Main Idea: God has intended that you enjoy your work.

Key Points:

To really enjoy your work fully, you:

- must enjoy the Lord,
- must have a compelling vision of what you do and why you do it,
- be realistic about work and the fruits of work,
- be realistic about thinking that you will change the world,
- be realistic about the length of your life,
- work on a positive attitude and do regular housecleaning on bad attitudes,
- must celebrate life and enjoy family and friends.

STUDY OR DISCUSSION QUESTIONS

1. Describe how you would like to feel about your work. Use at least four descriptive terms.

2. What obstacles keep you from feeling this way?

3. What could you do to enjoy your work more? What regular habits would help you?

4. Describe what a Christ-centered life would look like for you in your work circumstance.

5. List five realistic expectations that you could place on your career.

6. List five unrealistic expectations that people around you place on their work.

7. What are some practical things you could do to celebrate life with friends and family?

8. On a separate sheet of paper, write a few sentences or a short paragraph on a "compelling vision" for your work. Finish this point: Every day I go to work to . . .

9. How could you enjoy the Lord more?

10. At the beginning of this chapter, twelve terrible consequences of not having God at the center of your workday are listed. Can you add to the list?

— XI

DIAGNOSTICS

How blessed is the man who finds wisdom
And the man who gains understanding.
For its profit is better than the profit
    of silver,
And its gain is better than fine gold.
She is more precious than jewels;
And nothing you desire compares
    with her.
Long life is in her right hand;
In her left hand are riches and honor.

PROVERBS 3:13–16

W hen you are in the midst of practical problems, you want practical solutions. You want wisdom. The question is where do you get it?

THE LOST ART OF BIBLICAL WISDOM

In our culture today Christianity is making only a small dent in life. While churches are growing and attendance has been fairly high, problems still exist. But perhaps the greatest tragedy within the church is that work has become an invisible topic. Given the volume of Scripture that provides practical help on work issues, it is amazing that most pulpits in America will never address this topic in a sermon.

According to informal polls of twenty-five hundred people in Dallas, Boston, San Diego, and a few smaller cities, over 90 percent of all Christians have never heard a sermon on work, read a book on biblical principles related to work, or ever listened to a tape on the subject. Consequently, millions of Christians go to work every day, unaided and unchallenged by the Word of God as it relates to their work. The church is often silent on that part of life that takes up 60 percent of our waking hours, the place where we build the most bridges with non-Christians, and the area of life that profoundly affects the family.

As a result, many Christians have had to frame a philosophy of work and an approach to solving problems either on their own or from the avalanche of secular philosophy. Secular philosophy comes through seminars at companies, motivational programs, or books in the "self-help" sections of book stores. Often these sources dish up a plate of good ideas laced with anti-Christian values. A mature student of the Bible should be able to filter unbiblical aspects of the "human potential" and "new age" material. But the church's silence, coupled with the avalanche of secular ideas, often leaves Christians with only a secular rule book to follow.

But the Bible has volumes to say about work, as I hope you have already seen. This book has not come close to touching the depth of Bible wisdom about your work, your schoolhouse for applying practical wisdom. Now, the Bible cannot directly answer every problem that you face, but it contains thousands of principles that can enhance your ability to deal with work issues. My hope is that you will regard the Bible as your primary, daily source of wisdom for your work, that you will do your own study to solve the varied work issues you face. I urge you to be an active student of the Scriptures and to recover the lost art of applying biblical wisdom to your career issues.

THREE STEPS TO BIBLICAL WISDOM

Many work issues can be solved with the content of the previous chapters. But many specific questions are left to be considered. In this chapter we will look at ten common struggles and what to do about them. But before we jump to them, it would be good if we laid out a general procedure for solving work problems.

"Perhaps the greatest tragedy within the church is that work has become an invisible topic."

This process will involve three questions that can be asked of any work dilemma. You should ask these on the way to getting God's perspective on your attitude and actions.

Question #1: What Can I Learn or Gain from the Situation I Am In?

Chapter 2 discusses how your workplace can be a schoolhouse. In line with this, here are some specific subpoints that you can ask:

- What specific lesson can I learn from what I am facing?
- What biblical principle can I practice?
- What character lessons can I gain?
- How can this situation draw me closer to Christ?

The answers to these questions are well worth writing down and keeping in a journal. But they still don't deal directly with what you should do. That leads us to question 2.

Question #2: What Kind of Attitude Does God Want Me to Have Toward This Situation?

Here are some specific questions that you can ask yourself to get to the larger issue of what attitude God may want for you.

- What is my attitude now?
- What does God want it to be?

- What steps do I need to take to have this attitude?

Again, I urge you to write down your answers.

Question #3: What Action Steps Does God Want Me to Take?

As you know, the proper action is not always easy to determine. Sometimes I have wondered why there is no handwriting on the walls to tell us what God wants. Personally, I believe that in large measure God has already spoken to us in His Word, and He wants us to dig out the answers and develop the skill of applying them.

When our kids ask us how to spell or define a word, we often send them to the dictionary or encyclopedia for the answer. They are frustrated that we don't just come out with the answer, but we know that the process is just as important as the correct spelling. So the fact that you may struggle with what to do may well be a part of His plan to help you learn to seek His face and be more dependent on Him.

Let me suggest the following questions as a process for seeking what He would have you do.

- Are there any clear biblical commands that speak to your problem?
- Are there any biblical principles that relate to what you are facing?
- As you pray about what you should do, are there any impressions you have on your conscience?
- As you talk to other mature Christians about it, what do they say?

With this general process in mind, let's work toward answering some specifics. If you move through this process, you may be amazed at what comes out of it for you.

Now let us turn to ten recurring questions from people about their work. I have included questions I have heard over the last decade of speaking at conferences around the country. Each one could deserve a book in itself, so I hope you will understand that the response will be brief and as such not fully developed. But

---

"Instead of waiting for the job to become more interesting, you take a proactive role by putting more into it."

---

listed below is an approach to how you might begin to deal with these issues.

As you read the issues, be aware of the advantage to reading about problems that are not exactly the ones that you face. First, you may gain something from the method used. Second, you may want to be equipped to deal with these questions so you can help fellow believers in Christ who are struggling.

WHAT DO YOU DO WHEN YOU ARE IN A BORING OR UNCHALLENGING JOB?

There are three things you can do.

First, you can change your attitude about what you do. Perhaps you should review the chapter on God's view of your work. You may lack a compelling vision for what you do. Maybe you are angry at someone in your office, and it comes out as boredom. Ask yourself what attitude you would like to have. Then ask what attitude God would want you to have. Ask what could you do to develop a better attitude.

Next, you can find new ways to enhance your job and the contribution you make to your company. Let's say that you are a salesman for office products. You know that your product is needed, but you are bored with what you do all day. Sit down and list ten new and creative ways you could enhance the work and/or people you work with. Let me take a stab at what an office product salesperson could do.

1. Make a point of complimenting each client when you make calls.

2. Try to double the number of calls made on new prospects each month.

3. Begin to write thank you notes to each of your accounts.

4. Ask your boss what you could do to excel in your job.

5. Study professional material on being a good salesperson and practice one new idea a week.

6. Make sure each person you come in contact with feels appreciated and important to you.

7. Develop a list of ten questions you could ask your customers about how you could help them more. Then, approach a dozen or so with these and record their answers.

8. Meet with other sales people, and try to learn at least one sales tip from each of them.

9. Memorize Scripture between sales calls.

10. Get to know what each client's business is all about. If you are familiar with what the client does, try to double your knowledge.

Your list of suggestions might be different. But the point is to be creative to enrich your job. Instead of waiting for the job to become more interesting, you take a proactive role by putting more into it. Usually I find that a person who takes the time can think of ways to make it better.

Third, you can change jobs. Perhaps you could begin the process of looking for either a new job or a new career.

For this process I suggest a fine book, *Finding a Job You Can Love* by Ralph Mattson and Art Miller. It offers a self-test on finding out what motivates you. You can use the results as a guide when you think about your career direction.

HOW CAN YOU KEEP A GOOD ATTITUDE WHEN THE PEOPLE AROUND DO NOT?

Realistically all of us each day in the marketplace come against backbiting, complaining, anger, and excessive ambition. So every day we face a battle.

To fight these spiritual battles, you will want to equip yourself with every spiritual weapon. You will want to pray about temptations you face, asking God to keep you properly motivated, to guard your tongue, to keep your behavior right and pure. Renew your relationship with the Lord first thing each morning. This action might include:

1. Using the time driving into work to pray about your day and your attitude.

2. Reading Scripture before you go to work.

3. Meeting regularly with other Christians in your office complex to study God's view of work and how to honor Him.

4. Writing a biblical mission statement for your job.

5. Taking thirty-second prayer breaks at ten, two, and four.

6. Memorize important verses of the Bible that speak to issues you face.

In Christ we have all the resources to excel in the workplace and to be change agents rather than being pulled down to the level of others. But we must wage a daily battle. When we lose and give in to pressure around us, we simply need to confess it to God and move on.

I don't believe there is a way to make it easy. Living as a follower of Christ often implies that we live a rather lonely existence. Since it will be tough, we must not underestimate our need for daily spiritual preparation if we are to have spiritual victory.

WHAT DO YOU DO
WHEN THE WORK IS NEVER DONE?

You do your very best—and relax about the rest. You see, if you do your best, there is just enough time in every day to do what God wants you to do. If there is not enough time, then He must not have wanted it done. I have talked to many people who do their best yet feel bad every day about the work they did not finish. These wounded soldiers are conscientious workers who go home every night feeling they never reached the finish line.

But at some point most of us must accept His leadership in our lives—must realize that there is not enough time to do everything. When this happens, we are forced to set priorities, and even tradeoffs. Perhaps it would be better to do five jobs so-so than to do three jobs perfectly. This may not be to your liking, but you must decide what you are paid to do and what is best for your company and the customers.

Second, we must accept the fact that our best is good enough. We are just junior partners with God in our work. Unless He blesses our efforts, we are doomed to failure. Knowing that we have done what we could allows us the freedom to offer our work to Him in confidence that it will be good enough. If it is good enough for Him, it ought to be good enough for us.

Third, doing our best implies that we are organized in our work. This means setting priorities. If you think you have more than you can do, you need to ask the boss what his or her priorities are. Tell him that you are just trying to do your best and you want input.

Realistically, many of us will face this dilemma. Many companies are understaffed. Ten people may now have to do the work twelve used to. It may be a continual tension for you and require that you get God's perspective on your work each day. Remember the TRIALS acrostic.

WHEN SHOULD YOU LEAVE YOUR JOB?

If your only option is to compromise your integrity, you are on the wrong team. If your conscience bothers you about the work you are doing, then seriously consider leaving.

A few years ago, a manager of a drug store called me, concerned about his work. His store sold many fine items, and they also sold liquor. Every morning drunks lined up waiting for the

---

"Your best is good enough."

---

store to open. His conscience was killing him. It was time for him to do something else.

I believe that the sale, distribution, and promotion of tobacco are unethical for a Christian because they do not meet legitimate needs. Neither do I think a Christian should be involved in producing or selling radar detectors. Perhaps you can think of other careers that do not meet needs God wants to meet.

Beyond the ethical problems, you should review my remarks on leaving a job under the first question.

WHAT DO YOU DO
WHEN YOUR BEST WAS NOT GOOD ENOUGH?

If you have faced your best not being good enough, you know that it hurts a lot. You did your very best on the job, and you still got a low performance rating. You tried, but you did not make the sale. Even though you are a hard worker, you were laid off. You are a sharp business person, and your company still went under.

Your only hope for sanity is in a biblical perspective. Your best *is* good enough. You must accept that God did not choose to bless this particular project. You must allow God to be God in your life. The ultimate responsibility for your success lies in His hands, so you come to work holding your success with a light touch. You can and should work hard, with a passion for excellence, but He may have something better for you that you cannot see, and not blessing what you have may be a part of His plan. Remember that He does have a plan and it is a good one.

If you are going to have a pity party, have a short one and move on. One of the most important qualities of Christlike character is perseverance. Someone has said that there are two kinds of people in this world, those who have tasted failure and those who will. Failure is no one's favorite word, but it is common. When you face failure, it is important to focus on what you are going to do next.

Even if you continue to find that your best is not good enough in the same job, a job change is probably in order. So you can see why you must have more to your life than work.

WHAT DO YOU DO
WHEN YOU HAVE MADE A BIG MISTAKE?

Recently I was in a gas station paying for my gas and buying a diet soda. When I went to the counter, the young woman at the register rang up the gas but did not include the price of the soda. When I mentioned it to her she said, "Boy, am I stupid!" She said it with such self-hatred! I couldn't help but say, "You're not stupid. You just made a small mistake. That's why pencils have erasers."

But some of us take mistakes very hard. Others, perhaps, need to be a little more serious about them. Let's look at two kinds of mistakes: ethical and professional.

Few things are as painful to a Christian as an ethical mistake. Yet I do not know one follower of Christ who has not made several. Perhaps you lost your temper and said something you need to retract. Perhaps you took something that did not belong to you, such as an inflated business reimbursement. But integrity has two sides. First, we should strive to do the right thing. Second, when we stumble—and we all will—we should have the integrity to rectify and move on.

Recently, after a message I gave at a seminar for international students, I met a young couple from a South American country. They had just been married, but before the marriage they were

---

"Our integrity rests not just in doing the right things but also in taking responsibility for when we do not."

---

apart—she in Washington and he in South America. She had used the company phone to make several long distance calls to her fiancé. Later, after the talk on integrity, she realized that what she did was wrong and came to me and asked what she should do.

The first thing I encouraged her to do was confess it to God. Secondly, I reminded her that she must accept herself for what happened and not continue to feel condemned. God would not condemn her and neither should she.

But the hard part was making restitution for taking something that did not belong to her. She was worried that it might be laughed off by her superiors. She also was worried about what they would think and if this would give them an excuse for not becoming Christians. I urged her to see that our integrity rests not just in doing the right things but also in taking responsibility for when we do not. Ethical mistakes happen. Avoid making another one by taking proper action.

Professional mistakes happen too. Sometimes the mistake is enough to get a person fired. Other mistakes make you groan and slap your forehead in frustration. The important thing to keep in mind when a mistake is made, is to accept responsibility, accept yourself as imperfect, and move on. God is not shocked by mistakes. He "knows our frame." Don't allow yourself to be hindered from focusing on the work before you today. Remember to take one day at a time. You must move on and not be absorbed with self-anger or frustration.

A friend of mine is in commercial real estate. Because of the way he negotiated a piece of property for a client, the client lost a hundred thousand dollars. Of course, this put a lot of egg on my friend's face. Regrettable, certainly. But ultimately my friend works for a heavenly boss, and in His eyes, my friend is accepted, loved, and urged to move on.

When you make a mistake, write a short note in your "Lessons Learned" file and move on, "For a righteous man falls seven times, and rises again, but the wicked will stumble in time of calamity" (Proverbs 24:16).

WHAT DO YOU DO
WHEN YOU ARE A WOMAN IN A MAN'S WORLD?

Women who enter traditionally male-dominated fields find a host of issues. This subject deserves many good books. But for now, I would like to address two questions Christian working women have commonly asked me. The first question is "How can I retain a style that is feminine, in a world that values combativeness, aggressiveness, and dominance?"

Being "feminine" is largely a cultural concept framed in your thinking from your background. A traditionally feminine style of being nurturing and passive is far less appreciated in today's marketplace.

Generally, I urge men and women to compromise on preferences and stick to principles. Principles have to do with your integrity and represent your basic values. Preferences need to be on the table for negotiation as a servant and a person submissive to authority.

Many jobs require that men and women change their preferred behavior. All salespeople must learn to be more aggressive, to make "cold calls" and to face rejection. Managers must learn to be tough at times and less trusting of people. Your willingness to change, even if you don't like it, is a mark of your maturity.

A second question is, "How do I respond to sexual jokes, innuendoes and degrading remarks?" First, let me say that I am sure this is more difficult than I can understand, and I am sorry

---

*"Generally, . . . compromise on preferences
and stick to principles."*

---

the marketplace contains such injustice.

It seems, though, that the best advice I can give is to cultivate a long fuse and decide what are the boundaries or limits that mark unacceptable speech and behavior.

The crossing of some boundaries deserves a comment, a remark like, "That is unacceptable humor for me. I don't appreciate it."

Crossing some boundaries deserves a complaint to management. A repeated pattern of unacceptable behavior is worth such a complaint. A clear sexual invitation fits here as well.

Some boundaries are worth going to court for. Two extremes are worth noting. First, if you become a women's crusader, you may incite more negative behavior than you need to endure. On the other hand, don't be reluctant to speak up when it is appropriate. As always, I urge you to seek the Lord on what you should do in individual cases, and I hope these general remarks can help you frame your prayers and actions.

HOW DO YOU KEEP YOUR MOTIVATION HIGH IN THE FACE OF CUTBACKS AND PAY CUTS?

Obviously, layoffs and pay cuts will try your soul, but I encourage you to remember that your attitude is largely your choice. Certainly, complaining and worrying will be all around you. But you work for a different reason than most of your co-workers. You work for Jesus Christ, and you trust Him to meet your needs. You believe that if you do lose your job, He will take care of you and your family. You believe that He allowed the pay cutback in your life for your good.

Belief in these truths can make a big difference in your attitude. During times of such high stress, most people waste a large portion of their work potential. You can stay focused and positive because you continue to make Christ the center of every workday.

WHAT DO YOU DO
WHEN YOU FACE MIDLIFE DISAPPOINTMENT?

Please know up front that midlife disappointment is common, even among some of the most successful people. It seems that the changes going on in us during this phase may be as significant as the changes of puberty. The body is changing; your perception of life is changing. You are facing your own mortality for the first time. And often you are facing the harsh cold reality that life has not turned out as you thought it would.

In part, you will simply have to live through this period of life to get perspective on these feelings. Mistakes or false starts in your career may tend to haunt you. Questions about your significance arise too. But throughout an emotional storm, I urge you to keep a biblical perspective on your work and the results of your work each day. In large measure, I believe, midlife finally reveals the bankruptcy of our pride and our ego motivation for work. We see that competency, competitiveness, and consumption of luxury items are not all we thought they were.

But midlife is also a great place to make some midcourse corrections. Family may begin to mean more to us. We may become more serious about bringing Christ into our workday each day. We may become a little less self-absorbed and more committed to helping the next generation.

WHAT DO YOU DO
WHEN YOU HAVE LOST YOUR JOB?

The first thing you need to do if you have lost your job is make getting a new job your present job. In other words, make just as professional an effort to find a new job as you made on the job you had.

Don't allow yourself the opportunity to wallow ·in self-pity. Get up at the usual time and get dressed as you would for work. Get organized. Start with creating or updating a resume. Then begin to brainstorm all the opportunities you can think of for

---

"The first thing you need to do if you have lost your job is make getting a new job your present job."

---

your abilities. List people you know who might know of other opportunities.

Guard yourself against defeating ideas about your worth. Your worth and your job status have nothing to do with each other. During this time you will want to spend plenty of time in the Scriptures to combat any thinking that saps your confidence.

Getting a new job can be pretty exhausting and require a lot of courage. The Lord is the only source of real courage I know. If you believe that He loves you, that you are important in His eyes, that He will go before you on every job interview, and that He will give you what is best for you, then a "no" from a prospective employer means that God has something better for you. You sow the seeds, but trust God to make success happen and to lead you in the best direction. Getting the wrong job might be worse than delaying getting a job.

Review the TRIALS acrostic throughout your day. Realize that you will be vulnerable to negative thoughts like fear, unbelief, and anger. Keep your walk with Christ fresh each day. If you lose a job, you haven't lost much. If you lose something in your relationship with Christ, you have lost a lot!

The Scriptures must play a vital role in your life when things are going well and when they are not. Seeking the Lord for daily work issues should be a part of your habit pattern. You need the skill of applying the practical wisdom in His Word to life. If you do, you will make it!

> How blessed is the man who does not walk in the
>   counsel of the wicked,
> Nor stand in the path of sinners,
> Nor sit in the seat of scoffers!
>
> But His delight is in the Law of the LORD,
> And in His law He meditates day and night.
> And He will be like a tree firmly planted
>   by the streams of water,
> Which yields its fruit in its season,
> And its leaf does not wither;
> And in whatever he does, he prospers.
>
> (Psalm 1:1–3)

REVIEW

Main Idea: God's Word and biblical wisdom are applicable to a wide variety of work struggles.

Key Points:

- Three-step process for managing work difficulties:
    1. What can I learn or gain from this problem/situation?
    2. What kind of attitude does God want me to have?
    3. What action steps does God want me to take?

- Issues addressed in this chapter:
  1. when you are in a boring/unchallenging job
  2. keeping a good attitude when others don't
  3. when the work is never done
  4. when you should leave your job
  5. when your best was not good enough
  6. when you have made a mistake
  7. when you are a working woman in a man's world
  8. when you face cutbacks and layoffs
  9. when you face midlife disappointment
  10. when you have lost your job

STUDY OR DISCUSSION QUESTIONS

1. Take the three-step process and walk through a particular issue/problem you are facing.

2. What would you say to a person who had a problem and could not find any biblical guidance for it?

3. What are some of the ways you could maintain a good attitude if you lost your job today?

4. What could you add to the material in this chapter on:
   - how to enhance a boring job,
   - how to keep a good attitude,
   - what to do when the work is never done,
   - when you should leave your job,
   - when your best was not good enough,
   - when you made a mistake,
   - when you are facing sexual jokes and innuendoes,
   - keeping motivation high in the face of cutbacks and layoffs,
   - when facing midlife disappointment,
   - when you have lost your job?

PART 4

HONORING CHRIST UNDER PRESSURE

— XII

HEROES

*And he who overcomes, and he who
keeps my deeds until the end, to him I
will give authority over the nations.
He who overcomes, I will make him a
pillar in the temple of my God*

REVELATION 2:26; 3:12

When you think of a hero, what comes to mind? In the
Western world, few images present themselves on the
public scene. Many today lament the loss of "real" heroes.

Recently, Bill Moyers was interviewing Barbara Tuchman, a
nationally acclaimed historian here in Washington. Tuchman has
twice won the Pulitzer prize. In the interview, the topic of heroes
came up, and I so resonated with Ms. Tuchman's remarks that I
want you to read what she said.

First, she made the point that she wonders if our culture
would know a hero if it saw one.

> I was at a seminar a few weeks ago, down at the Smithsonian.
> They held a conference on the subject of the hero, because it was
> the fiftieth anniversary of the birth of Superman. I guess I
> should have realized, given the occasion for the conference, that
> what we would discuss would not be exactly my idea of a hero.
> And it certainly was not. It was quite weird, what they consid-
> ered a hero. The real hero of the discussion was the little girl
> who had fallen down a well. She didn't do anything to make

205

herself a hero; she was just in the news. Anyway, finally I got totally fed up and stood and said that they were confusing celebrity and notoriety with the word *hero,* and that this was not the definition of the word. (*A World of Ideas,* Bill Moyers, New York: Doubleday, 1990, 7)

This fiery woman went on to discuss what a real hero is. She included nobility of purpose, courage, and having a remarkable character. A hero is one who has an amazing belief in what is right and will prevail in spite of enormous frustration and difficulty. To Tuchman, George Washington was just such a man. She said of him:

He exerted an extraordinary quality of nobility that people felt just by being introduced to him, by seeing him, in spite of the terrible frustrations and difficulties that he faced when all the generals were pouring letters onto his desk telling him of their shortages—you know, no shoes, no money, no wagons to transport their food, and no food. . . .
Think of the decision to march his army all the way from New York to Washington—on foot—because he had made this arrangement to meet the French at the bottom of the Chesapeake to envelope [sic] Cornwallis. This was arranged across an ocean by letter. No telephone, no telegraphs, no satellites, no nothing, but letters. To think that he was able to do it on foot, and the French were able to come across an ocean and that Washington and the French met just as they planned. . . . It was a tremendous dare, which no one else would have ever been able to take, because no one else had the self-confidence that Washington had. (*A World of Ideas,* 9–10)

This whole discussion propels me out of my chair to shout *yes!* I agree. So much of what she reacts to hits the bull's-eye! Her understanding of George Washington squeezes out some real nectar concerning what a hero is. Nobility of purpose, *yes!* Perseverance in the face of incredible frustration, *yes!* Courage to take risks of reputation and even one's life for what is right, *yes!*

So what does this all have to do with you and me? Neither of us is likely to command an army or lead a nation. However, God has called us to be heroes too, not in some vague, small way but in a way far more significant to history than that of George Washington. Not the history that Ms. Tuchman and other excellent historians will write perhaps, but the history penned by the ultimate Writer of history, God Himself!

You see, heaven would agree with the qualities of heroism listed above. But God sees another aspect of heroes that men do not and cannot. God looks to ordinary people in ordinary circumstances to have extraordinary character.

ORDINARY PEOPLE

Somewhere the notion has filtered into our thinking that the hero club is for those few high-powered leaders who dramatically change the course of human history. George Washington was a

> *"Somewhere the notion has filtered into our thinking that the hero club is for those few high-powered leaders who dramatically change the course of human history. . . . But the heroes of the Bible had ordinary occupations. They were real; they sweated."*

man like this. But our mistake is that we think of only such high-visibility people in this category. We romanticize about human beings who are close to perfect and do not have the flaws that people like you and I have.

But the heroes of the Bible had ordinary occupations. They were real; they sweated. They were sheep farmers, slaves, a wine taster, fishermen, tax gatherers, carpenters, and the like. Most did agrarian work day and night. They faced drought, foreign conquest, and disease. Many were nomadic.

This noble group was far from perfect. David, the man the Bible said was "a man after God's own heart," was a murderer and an adulterer. He made a few other notable mistakes too. Moses was no saint either. He too murdered a man. He showed cowardice and came up with several excuses as to why he could not do what God wanted him to do with Pharaoh. Jacob was a liar, as was Abraham the father of the nation of Israel.

These men faced many ordinary issues. Daniel's peers were envious and tried to discredit him. Levi the tax gatherer was less popular than a dentist is today. Sheep were fed, masters were served, and so on. Ordinary people with ordinary jobs, with ordinary character flaws, doing ordinary tasks—these are the heroes in heaven's hall of fame.

But they had some extraordinary characteristics. Here are three important qualities that emerge from a study of their lives.

EXTRAORDINARY CHARACTER

Granted, these people are not perfect. If God needed perfect people He would never use anyone but His Son. But from His vantage, heroes display extraordinary life purpose in ordinary work problems and crises. Like George Washington, biblical heroes bear the distinguishing mark of noble purpose.

Every day they pursued an ideal of honoring God in their lives. Sure, like us they fell short. But they were after the highest and noblest purpose any man or woman could live for. They stumbled in following the ideal, but they got back up and continued. David, after being found guilty of murder and adultery, confessed His sin, took his discipline from God, and kept the faith. He continued to strive to know, honor and serve the Lord.

They too, like the American hero, persevered in difficult times and did not quit. Perhaps half of their lives were spent just persevering without any outward success. These men and women of the Bible lost their wealth, their health, their loved ones, their country, and their dignity. And yet each day they continued to pursue the noble goal.

Perseverance is one of the most magnificent qualities in an individual.

A few years ago I read about an athlete in an amateur triathlon. The swim was a mile long, the biking event was thirty-

---

"From [God's] vantage, heroes display extraordinary life purpose in ordinary work problems and crises."

---

eight miles of hilly terrain, and the run was 6.2 miles of hilly road surface in a hot summer sun. The athlete had lost both legs below the knees. Somehow the thought of his doing an event like that made me want to cry. I wondered if I had half the stuff he was made of.

But that is perseverance. It is a thing of beauty! In Christians perseverance shows up in many ways. For many people in tough circumstances, just showing up for work with a reasonably good attitude is a terrific victory.

The heroes of the Bible not only had nobility of purpose and perseverance, they had a passion to grow in their relationship with the living God. They pleaded with God to reveal His ways, His character, and His glory in a personal way. Paul said that he considered everything in life to be garbage compared to knowing Christ intimately. Moses begged God to reveal His glory to him. David asked when he had sinned that God might not take His Spirit from him. He asked to be restored to a right relationship with God. All of these ordinary heroes continually wanted to develop their relationship and were never satisfied. They had a holy greed to know God.

But ordinary people with extraordinary character are not an extinct breed of people that died out years ago. Today I know hundreds of such heroes. Let me tell you about some of them.

John

John had an everyday kind of job in a computer company. He worked hard and had a great reputation for being a loyal and hard worker. But when the company fell on hard times, he was fired. He is the father of three teenagers with a mortgage and all the normal costs of raising a family. He had been out of work for a few days when someone told me about his situation. When we met, I asked him how he was doing. He said that it was hard but that inside he knew that God would provide and that He must have something better for him.

A couple of months later I saw him, and there was still no job. But he had been diligent to get out each day and look for a job. His spirits were good. *It was tough, but he kept his head up.*

Shelley

Shelley is a secretary who works for a rather abusive boss. Each workday is not very pleasant. Her boss is selfish and demanding, and he looks down on women. He hasn't really sexually harassed her, but his jokes and his language with others in her earshot are offensive.

Even so, she feels called to work for this company. On her way to work she begs God for the right response to what she will face. She selects and reviews Scripture concerning her situation and tries to make each day a "win" in terms of pleasing the Lord. *It is tough, but Shelley keeps her head up!*

Rob

Rob has a responsible position in Washington. Outsiders would think he had it made, but his work is very tough. The bureaucratic nature of his work is terrible. Fundamentally, he does not like his job. But he really has no option to do something different until retirement. Every day Rob works on his attitude by reviewing God's perspective on his work. Especially, he will tell you that thanking God for the good things is a habit he has worked on. He will tell you that sometimes he complains. But more often than not he has the best attitude of anyone in his department, and people have told him so. He is a leader by virtue of his good attitude. I am so proud of him. *It is tough, but he keeps his head up!*

Barbara

Barbara is a physician—a surgeon actually. Recently, it looked as though her whole career was going to end because of a disease that threatened her ability to operate. She needed surgery and a

---

"I realize that I stand in the midst of a noble stream of men and women who have given their very lives to honor Christ."

---

long recovery period. Everything was up in the air for her. But day by day she focused on what God was doing in her life. She had no thought that this was punishment; she knew that God had allowed this pain for a reason, and she wanted to learn all she could from it. She told me that several good lessons came to her mind as she prayed and read the Scriptures. She has a real passion to grow. Living with the prospect of a future of pain, a derailed career, and other uncertainties *is tough, but she keeps her head up!*

These people and others like them are modern heroes. They may never win a trophy from mankind, but the glory they will receive from God is enormous. Their character is a thing of beauty! They are *real* heroes.

Real heroes inspire us; their demonstrated willingness to sacrifice leads us to higher ground. They have learned what is important and what is not. They have accepted pain and difficulty as a friend. They have struggled to make Christ the center of each workday. They have become learners in the schoolhouse of

Christlikeness. They know where their significance comes from. They have learned to trust God for the results of their work and lives. They have accepted God's leadership. They have persevered.

When things are tough or uncertain, I often begin to feel sorry for myself. Then I think of heroes. I realize that I stand in the midst of a noble stream of men and women who have given their very lives to honor Christ. They beckon me to follow their example and to imitate their faith. They persevered. They overcame. You and I must too!

One important advantage that these biblical heroes had was the knowledge that they would be rewarded generously for their faith. You, too, have a lot to look forward to. Let's look at some of your "second paycheck."

THE REWARD OF GLORY

It is humbling to receive a standing ovation. I have been through one. I didn't know who to look at, what to do with my hands, or whether to stand or sit. But it was wonderfully affirming.

Imagine the crowd around the throne of God, myriads of myriads of souls, a vast sea of heavenly creatures. You are standing there in the presence of Almighty God. It is the judgment seat of Christ (2 Corinthians 5). Your life is reviewed. The project you worked on at ten this morning, when you made a conscious effort to do it for the glory of God, receives a thunderous ovation, and the deep, powerful voice of God calls out, "Well done, My servant!" Next comes the ten-thirty event when you showed love to that difficult customer. Then the boss you forgave at eleven. Then the attitude of gratitude you worked on at lunch, and so on. In our time frame, you would receive years of such glory—real glory! Not the fleeting stuff of people who, for just a moment in time, catch a glimpse of who you really are.

The angels, the heavenly creatures, and the voice of God join in commending your every step of faithfulness to Him. It is almost too much to grasp. But wait, there's more.

THE REWARD OF RESPONSIBILITY

If heaven has a hierarchy of jobs, I see myself as shining shoes. Some of us will rule nations; others will lead heavenly hosts. Yes, there are eternal consequences to your attitude and actions at work and elsewhere. While little is clear about the details of the afterlife, it is clear that we will work for Christ and He will reward the faithful with responsibility.

This will bring about an amazing turnabout in the way things are. The street sweeper, who in a quiet way did his work for the glory of God will be a king. The shallow self-centered yuppie who sang to the Lord on Sunday and only congratulated himself during the week for his commitment to Christ, will sweep streets.

Some feel that even thinking about rewards leads to improper motivation. Not so—otherwise God would not have taken so much time in Scripture to promise rewards to the faithful. If it is okay to work for money, why not even more so for the "gold" we can take with us!

So how can our knowledge of these things work for us and inspire us to become "overcomers"? Two possibilities come to mind.

Cultivating an Awareness of Your Heavenly Audience

A recent study found that the number one fear in America is public speaking. Apparently, the thought of embarrassment is too painful for most people to want to face the opportunity.

Not to make you nervous, but imagine the audience watching us from heaven. Consider Hebrews 12:1: "Therefore, since we have so great a cloud of witnesses surrounding us, let us also lay aside every encumbrance, and the sin which so easily entangles us and let us run with endurance the race that is set before us." The "cloud of witnesses" referred to here are the heroes of the faith listed in Hebrews 11. The clear idea here is that the men and women who have gone on before you are standing in heaven to urge you on. These are the saints of whom it was said, "The world is not worthy."

Pretty amazing, isn't it? But there is much, much more.

Persevering: C'mon, Runner! You Can Do It!

If you have ever jogged or run in a race, you know that toward the end you just want to quit, to give in. It is so helpful to have people on your team cheering you on. But picture your heavenly Father urging you forward, reminding you of His love and of the glory before you for being faithful!

"You can be a hero; you must be a hero."

Imagine the Son reminding you that in Him you can have victory! He has set an example for you and promises you real meaning and purpose for the pain that you are enduring. Don't quit. Don't give in. Keep the faith!

Then there is the Holy Spirit, encouraging you—keep going, keep going. He is there to give you strength and victory over your old nature.

You can be a hero; you *must* be a hero. Men and women are in critical demand today to model for the next generation what it means to make Christ the center of each workday! You can be that person. My prayers are with you, and I hope this book will be an important resource to help you along your way.

You can only change a limited amount of your circumstances. With God's help you *can* change your attitude and have joy in the midst of chaos.

May God allow you the grace to enjoy Him and your work. God bless! I am cheering for you!

A THIRTY-DAY PLAN TO HELP YOU HONOR CHRIST AT WORK

I f you will simply dedicate five minutes every day for the next thirty days to the study of God's Word concerning your work, you can take an important step toward making Christ the center of each workday and enjoying your career. Follow the instructions after each day. You may want to put a check mark beside each assignment when completed, in order to mark your progress.

√ **Day 1**

Read Psalm 111. Underline every verse that portrays God as a worker. Then read Psalm 8 and study the high position God has given you as His junior partner. Why do you think God chose to give man such a position? What does this say about what you do all day?

Day 2

Read Ecclesiastes 1:1–11 and 2:18–23. Note how futile work is when God is left out of the picture and we just work for our egos.

Then see the conclusion the author comes to in 5:18–19. Take time to thank God for the gift of your job.

Day 3

Read Ecclesiastes 2:1–11 and 5:10–17. The author finds ego gratification from consumption of luxury to be short-lived. Study the passage and list four or five points the author makes.

Day 4

The need to impress man will keep you from pleasing God. Study the following texts to review this crucial concept. Galatians 1:10; Proverbs 29:25; John 12:42–43; John 5:44.

Day 5

Read Ephesians 6:5–8. List as many principles of work as you can find in it. This one passage will contain a wealth of wisdom for your work.

Day 6

Which is a more significant job in the kingdom of God—being a carpenter or a missionary? Read 1 Corinthians 7:20–22. Why do you think many are confused about this?

Day 7

Read Matthew 22:37–39. How can you love Christ more in your work? How can you love your co-worker more than you do yourself?

Day 8

A purpose of work is to give. Ephesians 4:28. What limits could be set on your lifestyle to increase your giving in the future? What percentage of your income do you give away? How do you feel about it?

Day 9

If your *real* boss is Jesus Christ (Colossians 3:23), how would that change your work habits?

Day 10

Read 1 Corinthians 15:5. If your job is part of "the work of the Lord," what is commanded here? Read Ephesians 6:5–8 again. What do these passages say about being rewarded by God for good work? Reread your career statement.

Day 11

What are the benefits of having integrity? Read Psalm 15:12; Proverbs 10:9; 12:19; 16:7; 28:6.

Day 12

Throughout your day today, you will talk to many people. Note what God says about your speech. Ephesians 4:29–30. Also James 3:2–12.

Day 13

Read Psalm 15 and list principles of biblical integrity.

Day 14

How did God view deceit and lying in the early church? Acts 4:32–5:11. Why was the consequence so drastic?

Day 15

Read Romans 12:17–21. What are some subtle ways angry people seek revenge (e.g., showing up late for a meeting)?

Day 16

Read Romans 12:2. How can you avoid picking up the attitudes, values, and behavior of those around you?

Day 17

What is the price of compromise? What is the price of integrity in your career? Which is higher?

Day 18

Read Ephesians 6:12. What are some practical habits you should have every day to take up the full armor of God?

Day 19

Reconsider your career statement. Would you like to enhance any part of it? If so, do it today.

Day 20

Read 1 Corinthians 13. How could this passage relate to your relationship to three of your co-workers? List their names and some thoughts from the passage.

Day 21

Read Psalm 127:1–2. How would you describe God's role in the success of your day today? Take a moment to ask Him for help in the major aspects of your workday today. Pause at 10:00 A.M., 2:00 P.M., 4:00 P.M. for thirty seconds and ask him for help; for wisdom, self-control, enthusiasm, insight, and power. Review the TRIALS acrostic.

Day 22

Read James 4:13–16. Why is the phrase "If the Lord wills" so important to God?

Day 23

How could stress, anxiety, and a fear of the future indicate improper motivation at work? Review the TRIALS acrostic.

Day 24

What would you say to an alcoholic who drowns his work difficulties with alcohol? Do you use any escape mechanism to run from work trials?

Day 25

Read Psalm 77:7–10, and list the questions Asaph asked God. Then read vv. 11–15 to study what changed his attitude. Review the TRIALS acrostic.

Day 26

Read Colossians 1:9–11, and note what Paul prayed for them. Pray these things for yourself, particularly as they apply to your work today.

Day 27

List the ten most valuable gifts God has given you and take some time to thank him for them. Review the TRIALS acrostic.

Day 28

List five events in your past where God clearly led you or protected or blessed you.

Day 29

What is the thing in the future you are most nervous about? Read Matthew 6:33–34 and Philippians 4:6–7. Take time to pray about it. Review the TRIALS acrostic.

Day 30

Read Philippians 3:8–14. Ask God to give you a passion to experience, honor, and proclaim Christ.

SUBJECT INDEX

A

Abraham 22, 208
Adam 62
alcohol 19–20, 42, 47, 180, 219
ambition 11, 25, 103
attitude 3, 11, 17, 19–20, 24, 33, 59,
   66–67, 73–74, 85, 98, 113, 119–120,
   122, 124, 139–140, 142, 145, 147,
   168–169, 173, 178–179, 181, 187,
   189, 191, 197, 200–201, 209–210,
   212, 214, 217, 219

B

biblical wisdom 186
bitterness 9, 11, 13, 18, 126–127, 129,
   132–133, 138, 145, 148

C

Career Impact Ministries 2
character 17, 21–22, 26, 29–30, 32–33,
   35, 104, 112, 129, 147, 187
character transformation 3, 17–18
Christian working women 196, 201
co-workers 13, 19, 40, 56, 73–74, 78,
   117–120, 122, 129, 132–133, 135,
   139, 142, 149, 178, 197, 216, 218
common ground 13–16
compelling vision 173
competent 48–49, 55–56, 59, 78, 170,
   198
competing time demands 157
conflict 128, 132–133, 164

D

daily focus 102, 104, 107–108, 171, 191
Daniel 22, 208
David 22, 208–209
depression 16, 19
desire for creative fulfillment 40
desire for personal significance 41–42,
   60, 84, 88
detached 15, 19–20
difficult boss 135–136, 138
do all you can 131–132
don't go to sleep angry 123–124, 132
drugs 14, 20, 42

E

ego biscuits 42, 44, 46–47, 52, 54–55,
   59, 72, 78, 118, 124, 170, 215–216
ego stress 153–154
enjoy your work 168
escape hatches 14–15, 91, 175
eternal life 79
ethical mistake 194–195

F

faces of pain 9
faith 4, 12, 47, 79, 83, 88, 93, 100–102,
   107, 112, 141, 144, 147, 158, 175,
   208, 213–214
fear of criticism 88–91
fear of embarrassment 88, 90–91, 213
fear of failure 88

fear of insignificance 41, 52, 78, 87–88, 90–91, 93–94, 155, 180
fear of rejection 52, 90–91, 93, 180
Finding a Job You Can Love 190
Flip Wilson 127
forgiveness 26, 84, 123, 125
friends 163
frustration with God 14

G

go the extra mile 130–132
goals 157, 165
God is a worker 60
grateful 100
Great Commandments 70
grow 26, 109

H

Habakkuk 104, 106
heroes 22, 205–209, 211, 214
holding on too tightly 154–155, 165
How to Balance Competing Time Demands 162
How to Succeed Where It Really Counts 155
hypocrites 10

I

imitation of Christ 29
immoral sex or sexual fantasies 14, 19–20
impact on others 30
impress others 67–68, 73
inner peace—contentment 27–29, 95
intimacy with Christ 29
Israel 105

J

Jacob 208
James 123, 182, 189
Job 22, 104
Joseph 22, 142–143
joy as a choice 167–168, 178

Joy of Stress 43
Judah 105
junior partner 71–72
justice-mercy continuum 142, 144, 148

K

King Solomon 22, 170, 180
Kipling, Rudyard 27, 170
Kushner, Harold 29

L

Levi 208
Lewis, C. S. 23, 31
life management 162, 165
Luther, Martin 64
luxury 49, 55, 59, 78, 198, 216

M

Mattson, Ralph 190
Miller, Art 190
miracles 98, 101
Moses 22, 208–209
Moyers, Bill 205

N

Nebuchadnezzar 104, 106
new job 199
New Rules 175
not paying 144

O

opportunity knocking 3, 12, 16, 18
organization 159
overeating 14, 19

P

Paul, Apostle 24, 28–29, 68, 72, 82, 137, 209, 219
perseverance 208–209, 212
personal significance—worth 79–80
Pettler, Pamela 43
pornography 14, 19–20

positive change 16, 26
Powers, Gary 40
pride 12, 79, 118, 123–124, 164, 198
prioritizing 159–160, 165–166
Problem of Pain, The 24, 31
procrastinating 158, 164
professional mistakes 195
Pursuit of God, The 99, 172

R

radically new perspective 60
reconciliation 127, 132
reputation 147
rest 162, 166, 192
revenge 13, 129, 132, 138
reward of glory 212
reward of responsibility 213

S

self-acceptance 86–90, 92, 94–95
service to others—servants 64–65,
   67, 74, 110, 136, 139, 162, 174, 196,
   212
slandering 146
strategies at work 40, 54
strategy 43, 45–50, 55
stress 3, 9, 20, 33, 40, 46, 50–51, 78,
   151–153, 155–156, 158–160, 164–
   166, 198, 218
Success 52
sued 144
super mom 156, 158

T

take charge 32, 34
take heart 31, 34
take notice 30, 34
take time 32, 34
television as a drug 14, 19–20, 110
third desire 41
Tozer, A. W. 1, 99, 172
trials 16–17, 24–25, 102
TRIALS acrostic 96, 109, 111, 113,
   139, 199, 218–219
Tuchman, Barbara 205, 207

V

vision of the future 106

W

Wall Street Journal 129
Washington, George 206–208
wisdom 3, 34, 69–70, 73, 79, 105, 119,
   200, 216, 218
work difficulties 3, 9, 17, 200
work issues 9, 185–186, 200
work struggles 13, 18
work through conflict 122
workplace 21
World of Ideas, A 206
worth to God 81, 83, 92

Y

you are his co-worker 62
Your Work Matters To God 10

SCRIPTURE INDEX

Genesis

1:16	60
1:21	60
1:26	62
1:7	60
2:2	60
3:17b–19	176
45:5–8	143
50:20	143

Exodus

20:8–11	162
20:9	61

Numbers

11:4–6, 10	99

Nehemiah

9:17	102

Job

38:2–4, 12, 18, 34	105

Psalm

1:1–3	200
8:3–6	63
8:5	80
75:6–7	145
77:7–9	14
78:40–43	102
103:11–14	84
103:15–16	53
104:14	61
105:4	71
111:2–6a	61
139:1–4	81
139:17–18	82
139:18–19	82
139:23–24	33

Proverbs

15:1	125, 128
6:6–8	159
15:18	128
16:32	129
24:16	196
24:30–34	158

Ecclesiastes

1:15	174
2:11	171
5:10	50
5:15	177
7:20	177
9:7–8	180
9:9	181

Daniel

4:34, 35	106

Habakkuk

3:17–18	106

Matthew

5:23–25	128
5:38–41	131
6:11	102
6:34	107
22:36–39	64
26:52	138

Luke

6:35–36	119
6:35b	118

John

4:34	67
5:44	137
8:54	66

Romans

1:26	80
5:3–5	23
8:1	85
8:33, 35	85
12:3	72
12:17, 19	130

Galatians

5:22	22, 167

Ephesians

4:26	126
6:8	68

Philippians

2:14–15	120

3:1	167
3:12–14	29
4:5	140
4:8	181
4:11, 12	29

Colossians

3:23–24	64

1 Corinthians

4:7	86
10:1–11	101

2 Corinthians

1:8–9	24

Hebrews

12:1	213
12:14–15	126
13:5	85
13:8	102

James

1:2–4	167
3:5–6	146
4:1, 2	123
4:13–16	109

1 Peter

2:18	139
2:18–21	137

Revelation

3:7	104

ABOUT
THE AUTHOR

D oug Sherman is a leading spokesman on "the Christian and
the workplace" and is the founder and president of Career
Impact Ministries. CIM is an organization dedicated to challeng-
ing this generation to put Christ at the center of each workday.
He travels extensively speaking on this topic and has written four
books including *Your Work Matters to God.*

He is a graduate of the United States Air Force Academy and
served as a flight training instructor. He also had experience in
sales and marketing prior to attending Dallas Theological Semi-
nary where he obtained a master of theology degree. Doug and his
wife Jan and three children reside in the Washington, D.C., area.

To obtain information about how Career Impact Ministries
can help you, call their toll-free number 1-800-4IMPACT.

The typeface for the text of this book is *Palatino*. This type—best known as a contemporary *italic* typeface—was a post-World War II design crafted by the talented young German calligrapher Hermann Zapf. For inspiration, Zapf drew upon the writing legacy of a group of Italian Renaissance writing masters, in which the typeface's namesake, Giovanni Battista Palatino, was numbered. Giovanni Palatino's *Libro nuovo d'imparare a scrivera* was published in Rome in 1540 and became one of the most used, wide-ranging writing manuals of the sixteenth century. Zapf was an apt student of the European masters, and contemporary *Palatino* is one of his contributions to modern typography.

Substantive Editing:
Michael S. Hyatt

Copy Editing:
Donna Sherwood

Cover Design:
Steve Diggs & Friends
Nashville, Tennessee

Page Composition:
Xerox Ventura Publisher
Printware 720 IQ Laser Printer

Printing and Binding:
Maple-Vail Printing Group
York, Pennsylvania

Cover Printing:
Strine Printing Company
York, Pennsylvania